CONFESSION AND AVOIDANCE

LEON JAWORSKI
with Mickey Herskowitz

Confession and Avoidance

A MEMOIR

Anchor Press/Doubleday
Garden City, New York
1979

ISBN: 0-385-13440-1
Library of Congress Catalog Card Number: 77-16926

To Joe,
a top trial lawyer in his own right;
and to Mike,
who would have been,
this book is affectionately dedicated

ABOUT THE TITLE

Historically, lawyers have made occasional and careful use of a legal term called *Confession and Avoidance:* The defendant did the act, but should be excused for legal or moral reasons.

There are other definitions, but this is the one I prefer. No lawyer writes lightly about a lifetime at the bar. When one undertakes such a task, his plea necessarily should be one of confession and avoidance.

Grateful acknowledgment is due to partners, associates, and staff members who rendered assistance in the course of the endeavors recounted herein; to my family and friends who encouraged the writing of this book, and to Connie Dillon Hutchison for her proficient secretarial services.

Contents

1
Salad Days

When the postcard came I was puzzled by its timing. Only a few weeks before, I had finished my role in the investigation of the Korean influence scandal. Watergate was four years behind me. But no matter. The postcard, mailed from a small town in Florida, was signed by an old Baylor University classmate, a man I probably had not seen in fifty years.

In its entirety, the card read:

> Dear Leon:
>
> The morning after you were named Special Prosecutor in the Nixon case, I went around town talking to people and saying, "My chief claim to fame is that I had English 103 with Mr. Leon Jaworski." When I used this on my barber, he replied: "That's nothing; I went to the same high school as O. J. Simpson."

I will forgo any other statement about the American way of fame, about lawyers and football players and how we see

ourselves. Fame is not a long-term investment. Facts are
the lawyer's commodity. How he gathers and uses them,
how he prepares a case and then presents it, the manner he
adopts, all are part of the lawyer's art.

By nature or design, each of us cultivates a style. I would
be a poor one to describe mine, but this I know: I have no
patience with minutiae. I have spent my life cutting
through trivia, getting to the core of a story. Maybe this is
why I have read, from beginning to end, only two long
novels in my lifetime: Gone With the Wind and Dr.
Zhivago. As a boy, I was always in a hurry to see what
was around the next corner.

I was born with a muffin face, which is not the sort of
thing one would usually complain about. But when I
began to practice law at the age of twenty, and looked
much younger, my appearance did not favor me.

More than most attorneys of that time, I learned to exercise care about how I dressed and acted. Many jurors were
unsympathetic to me at the start of a trial. I had to win
them over. If they could not accept me, how could they accept the rightness of my client's position?

My clothes were conservative, never flashy. I worked at
keeping my face impassive. I would never smoke a cigar in
court, lest I come across as a smart aleck or a show-off. In
many courtrooms today, of course, smoking is no longer
permitted, not even by spectators. But in those days—the
1920s and 1930s—lawyers frequently chewed tobacco in
court, as well as smoking it.

Many a time I have lectured my firm's young lawyers on
the realities of trial by jury: too often they will be judged,

and not the facts. Too often lawyers will ruin a case by
their own demeanor, and by ignoring the warning signals
that can be observed in the eyes of the jurors.

The trial of cases in 1979 is not what it was in 1929.
Over that half of a century, the nature of litigation, as well
as the dramatics—the gripping episodes of unexpected
events as the lawsuit unfolded—has vastly changed. This is
true both in criminal and civil cases. Whether this means
that there is now a greater sense of justice in our system is
debatable.

In a personal way, I mourn the passing of that era, and
the fencing that went on between opposing counsel that
was so basic to the art a lawyer could employ. The unexpected thrust of a question on cross-examination often
affected the credibility of a witness. Today the requirement
of pretrial disclosures usually enables both sides to be fore-
warned on what to expect when the witness takes the
stand. In criminal cases, the idea, fashioned by court decision and legislative fiat, and noble in theory, is that the accused should know what confronts him. In most cases, a
lawyer today infrequently knows the exquisite pleasure of
"springing a trap" for the lying or deceitful witness.

I began my legal career more than fifty years ago, at a
time when the rules were simpler, the traditions clearer
and unquestioned. I was drawn to law by the simple discovery that it was a natural haven for a boy with ideals who
liked to argue. My father had instilled in his four children
a desire to achieve. We needed to excel, in school and in
our private conduct, to win the acceptance of those who
mocked anyone with a foreign name and a different accent.

In our home, in Waco, Texas, German was the language of my father and stepmother. In the years during, and immediately after, World War I, anti-German and anti-immigrant feeling ran high in small towns across the land.

I had thought I might study medicine, as my older brother, Hannibal, did. In his teens, Hannibal—I called him "Bo," and still do—worked as an orderly at the local hospital. He became known as Joe to the nurses and other staff people who found Hannibal Jaworski too forbidding a name. Later, when he returned to the same hospital as a physician, they simply elevated him to "Doctor Joe," a name he is still known by in Waco.

But in my junior year I won a high school debating championship. The next year I won again. My classmates at Waco High, and their families, seemed friendlier. I changed my mind about becoming a doctor.

I thought then that the law offered an opportunity halfway between medicine and the ministry. Some kind of idealism is essential to the lawyer's fulfillment of his duties, and I have tried over the years not to lose mine.

The law is always in transition, walking a tightrope between precedent and social change. What remains the same is the greatest of all obligations borne by the lawyer—that of unswerving loyalty to the ends of justice. Not justice for the affluent and the powerful alone, not justice for the admired and the favored alone, not justice for those whose views and beliefs are shared, but justice for the weak, for the poor, and even for the hated.

In the weeks after World War II, American officers—lawyers in civilian life—admirably defended the accused in war crimes trials held in Germany. Some of the crimes were as barbarous as any in history. Yet American lawyers, to their everlasting credit, fought vigorously and tenaciously to make certain that the accused received due process.

Granting justice to the unpopular cause is a problem that exists today, perhaps more so than a decade ago, surely more so than at the turn of the century. There is a growing tendency of some of the most capable members of the Bar to shun the representation of those in public disfavor. Quickly forgotten, or lightly taken, appears to be the oath of the lawyer. When entering his profession, a lawyer does not engage in a popularity contest. He accepts a special obligation—as the late Mr. Justice Jackson put it—"to safeguard every man's right to a fair trial."

Not all cases are historic or dramatic, the typical lawyer driven and colorless, his preparations grim and tedious. Every lawyer has his theatrical moments. Arguments to the jury are, in the best sense, a monologue. The cross-examination is often no less than a scene played out by two actors. A lawyer needs ego. It is one's armor. A person's ego gets things done . . . if kept under control.

My first law partner, and mentor, was a man named Tom Scott, in Waco, a gifted storyteller. One of his stories involved a fellow Waco lawyer who had been appointed by the court to defend a man charged with not one but several cases of murder. For weeks after the trial, this defense counsel buttonholed friends and acquaintances on the sidewalks, or in other public places, and regaled them with the highlights of his performance: how he had outwitted the

district attorney, how skillfully he had cross-examined the
state's witnesses.

Inevitably, his captive listener would ask, "Well, what
happened to your client?" The lawyer paused, and then answered, absently, "Oh, him. Him they hung."

I was still in my salad days in Waco, in 1928, when I received a call from a man who identified himself as Charlie
Allison, of Fort Worth. A mutual friend had recommended me, he said. I had successfully defended a number
of bootleggers, although the county was dry and Prohibition was in full roar. Allison asked me to represent him in a
case pending in El Paso, against a charge of conspiracy to
violate the liquor laws.

The Volstead Act was the law of the land. The enemies
of drinking were, and in some places still are, persistent
and sincere. But so are its fans. Allison was charged, along
with others, with hauling alcohol from Mexico into Texas.
Since time was short, I arranged to meet with him on a
Sunday afternoon in my office.

At the precise moment we had agreed on, the door
opened. Allison was tough-looking, leathery, uneducated,
known as the king of the bootleggers in North Texas. He
had a reputation, he told me, for doing quality work. The
alcohol he smuggled across the border was then mixed, bot-
tled attractively, and sold as Bourbon. He had become
wealthy as a result of his enterprises.

A tragic event had led to the conspiracy charge. According to the story Allison unfolded, one of his cohorts, a
young man, had been caught on the Texas side of the bor-

der with a number of large cans of alcohol piled into his automobile, a Model A Ford coupe with a turtleback. The car was a popular one among those trafficking in alcohol.

When the young man was stopped and arrested, he asked for permission to smoke a cigarette. Instead, he drew a small pistol and at point-blank range shot the officer, a veteran of many years and widely admired by those who knew him. He later died. The act was cruel and brainless and had the effect of outraging law officers all over the state.

But the suspected killer escaped and could not be found. There was proof that he worked with my client, and the police were determined to convict Allison unless he was willing to reveal the whereabouts of his confederate.

Allison laid down the story in detail. He said he had other attorneys in Fort Worth, but had lost confidence in them. He asked me to take charge of the case; then he asked about my fee. Without hesitation, I told him it would be worth $1,000. If one were to compare that figure to today's prices, it would be like asking for your weight in emeralds, given fifty years of inflation and the shrinkage of the dollar.

Allison did not bat an eye. He excused himself and left the building. His wife was waiting in the car with their checkbook. In a moment he was back. Without a word he handed me the check. It was my first "big" fee, the details of which no lawyer ever forgets.

We agreed to meet in three days in Fort Worth, where I would review the case with his other lawyers. After he left I waited a few minutes, then pressed the button for the only

elevator. When the door clanked open, the boy running
the elevator greeted me with a wide grin and said, "Mr. Jaworski, all I want to ask you is if that check was really for
$1,000?"

In Fort Worth, I met with his lawyers and was appalled
at the lack of strategy. Allison and I decided to drive immediately to El Paso, allowing ample time to prepare for the
trial. The trip was long and boring, or should have been—
expressways were unknown then. We were seated in the
rear of his Cadillac, driven by a chauffeur who had been in
his employ for some time. When we came to an isolated
area, several hours out of Fort Worth, Allison leaned forward and warned his driver to proceed with caution. I next
noticed that my client had pulled out a pistol, either from
his pocket or from under the seat, and was holding it on
his knee, in an upright position.

My face must have revealed my concern, because he
quickly explained that this was the area in which automo-
biles and trucks containing alcohol hauled from Mexico
frequently were stopped and, as he put it, heisted. Obviously, those engaged in the illegal transportation could not
complain, and this soon proved to be a racket. It was not a
very comfortable feeling to be sitting next to someone
holding a pistol at the ready. There was no incident, however, and after we reached El Paso I went straight to the
office of the United States attorney.

I needed to determine what disposition could be made
of Allison's case, or whether we would proceed to trial. As
it turned out, what the authorities in El Paso were most interested in was to have my client reveal the whereabouts of

the young fellow who had shot and killed the customs officer. The U.S. attorney offered to dismiss the case against Allison, provided he gave them the information.

Allison thought it over. I was not aware of it until later, but he had been taking care of this fugitive and his family. Finally, he said to me that he believed he should reveal his whereabouts. He disapproved of the violent act that had taken place, he said. He had always told his men, if they were caught, not to resist arrest. Charlie seemed honestly distressed that an officer had lost his life.

He knew where the suspect had fled. But he was not an articulate man, and his efforts to tell the U.S. attorney the exact point in Oklahoma did not go smoothly. The law officers studied a map and kept trying to locate the spot Allison had described. For a while they suspected he was misleading them. Indeed, his former cohort was hiding out at a dog kennel in a fairly remote area. Finally, the officers were able to pinpoint the place that Allison had in mind. I was told that his charges would be dismissed.

We were on the road to Fort Worth the next day when we heard over the car radio that officers had captured their man in Oklahoma. They were returning him to Texas when, according to the news report, he broke away from one of his guards and tried to escape. He was shot and killed.

Charlie Allison continued to live in Fort Worth and from time to time pursued his interest in the liquor business. One evening a shotgun blast was fired into the window of his sitting room. It left Allison disabled, with a withered arm.

For better or worse, no matter how short the contact or how flawed the character, a lawyer often develops an empathy with his client. It is basic to the profession that no one seeks your services unless he or she is in trouble, has a problem or a grievance. The vulnerable, not the strong, knock on an attorney's door.

I last saw Charlie Allison after I had been in Houston and practiced there for several years. He walked in one afternoon, unannounced, and asked me for money.

This was after the repeal of Prohibition. Human experience had shown us that drinking could be made unlawful, it could even be condemned as un-American, but it was mainly unavoidable. Repeal had removed Charlie, and others like him, from the bootlegging business. Charlie knew no other work. He was, I would shortly learn, trying to break into a new and uglier game.

It was difficult to believe that this man, in whose long Cadillac I had ridden, who had been wealthy and secure and hard-natured, was now broke and begging. His clothes were shabby. The skin of his face sagged and he needed a shave. The arm hung limply at his side.

Sadly, he told me that he had a place where he could buy drugs. I gathered he would resell them for a profit and make a new start. I suspected also that he had an addiction of his own.

I told Allison I would gladly leave the office with him and would buy food and clothing and whatever else he needed. But I could not give him money to peddle drugs. I tried in vain to convince him that I wanted to help. But there was no way I could encourage him, or participate with him, in the venture he proposed.

He glared at me for a long time, long enough for me to remember the gun sitting upright on his knee in the back seat of the car. Without another word he turned around and walked out of my office. I never saw him again.

Most criminal lawyers either develop a protectively thick skin or doom themselves to a lifetime of sleeping potions and stomach remedies. No matter how the case ends, although the client may be going to prison or beyond, a lawyer is only going back to the office.

I was influenced at a critical point in my career by John H. Crooker, Sr., the founding partner of what is now the firm of Fulbright and Jaworski.

The firm was called Fulbright, Crooker, Freeman and Bates when I opposed it in one of my first cases after arriving in Houston. I was twenty-four, pitted against two of the name partners in my future law firm, John H. Freeman and Colonel William B. Bates. They were representing their biggest client, and the issue was whether it owed one of the clients of A. D. Dyess, my boss, $10,000 plus interest —a substantial sum of money in those days.

Dyess, a great trial lawyer in jury cases, had won the verdict earlier, and I was seeking to uphold it in the Court of Civil Appeals, in Galveston. Although the court did not convene until 9:30 A.M., I was there by 7:30 A.M., as nervous as a cat in a room filled with rocking chairs, wondering what fate would befall me.

As the docket was being called, two gentlemen walked in

and sat directly behind me. I heard one say to the other, "I
don't see Dyess anywhere." This indicated to me that one
or the other was my adversary, and I turned around and introduced myself. Freeman turned to Bates and said, simply, "Dyess must not think much of his lawsuit." The comment not only startled but offended me, and much of the
nervousness I had experienced just vanished.

Freeman and I argued the case and locked horns rather
hotly on certain points. The Court upheld the judgment
Dyess obtained in the lower court.

No one in my professional life was to be dearer to me
than John H. Freeman. A year later he offered me a job, at
considerably more money than I was making. It was an
offer that any other twenty-five-year-old trial lawyer in
Texas would have found impossible to refuse. But I kept
putting off Freeman. Finally he took me in to see John
Crooker, Sr.

"What the hell's the matter with you?" Crooker raged,
in his usual straightforward fashion. "Any lawyer in Houston would give anything to join our law firm, but you keep
fartin' around."

"Mr. Crooker," I said, "you've got two fair-haired boys
here already"—there was no need to name them—"and
they both have strong family connections. I don't know
anybody and I don't want to go up against that. I can't
bring you any business."

"Listen," Crooker retorted, "we don't need anyone to
bring us business. We need someone to attend to it." A
few days later I went to work for the firm that would one
day bear my name.

On more than one occasion, as Crooker and I strolled to the courthouse to begin a trial, he would comment: "Well, Leon, I am taking my twenty-five years of experience into the courtroom with me today and you will have to supply the rest." I knew what he meant. His experience, and my preparation, would do the job.

While still a young lawyer in Houston, I tried a number of cases in the court of a judge I admired. He was very able, but had become quite elderly. It was not unusual for him to fall asleep during the course of a trial, or in the middle of a legal argument or motion.

One day to my chagrin, as I argued a point important to my case, the judge began to snore. I had several law books on a table in front of me. One was as thick as the kind of universal dictionary one finds in the public library. I picked it up, began to read an excerpt that upheld my position, and then deliberately let it slip from my fingers and fall to the floor. The thud was enough to awaken his honor, and I had his attention the balance of the argument.

A lawyer can't hesitate to put his own neck on the line in defense of a client, nor should he become so in love with his own voice that he misses the natural humor of the courtroom. A lawyer who appears startled, who doesn't know why the jury laughed, has wasted precious currency.

I have faced my share of judges and jurors. I know that cases can be lost by a move badly timed, a question unasked, a word misused or misread. It is not a business where one can gaze out windows and succeed.

At the risk of sounding incurably romantic, I must admit that I have developed a feeling for the law that is close to love. Most of my friends are lawyers. I admire them. Lawyers do their most crucial work before your eyes and are bound by a code of respect and courtesy not found in most other professions.

Such words may sound hollow, even hypocritical, to those who have seen opposing lawyers clash and bait each other. I am sure I have appeared close to blows with an adversary in whose office I would later lift a glass of cheer while the jury considered its verdict.

At one point during the Watergate case, I was cornered by a very agitated Charles Rhyne, the attorney for Rose Mary Woods, who was then being questioned on the famous eighteen-and-a-half-minute gap in one of the Nixon tapes. Rhyne is an old friend, and a former president of the American Bar Association, as I was. But he felt his client had been abused and he came at me, waving a transcript of a meeting held—before he had been engaged—in the chambers of Judge John J. Sirica. The meeting had been attended, among others, by myself and the White House counsel, J. Fred Buzhardt.

Rhyne was muttering about the unfairness of comments relating to Rose Mary Woods. I told him that I could recall nothing that had been said in this conference that was unfair to her, or even accusatory. Raising his voice, Rhyne demanded, "What do you mean? Look here. Here we have Buzhardt saying, 'I am disgusted with Rose Mary Woods.' "

The tone of his voice, the expression on his face, demanded satisfaction. The implication was clear. If the White House was "disgusted" with her, then Rose Mary

Woods was being offered up as the perpetrator of that mysterious gap.

He repeated the statement attributed to Buzhardt. I said, "Well, Charlie, I can only tell you that nothing like that was said."

"Then I think we ought to get to the bottom of it," he demanded.

The comment to which Rhyne objected simply did not ring true. I studied the transcript again. Then it hit me, and I laughed out loud. The look on Charlie's face changed from pained to quizzical.

"That isn't what Buzhardt said," I told him. "His words were, 'I have not *discussed* this with Rose Mary Woods.'" The court reporter had garbled the sentence.

Some disputes, I thought to myself, are just easier to solve than others.

2
Poor Man

Over the years, I have changed my mind half a dozen times on the issue of capital punishment. But as an impatient young lawyer, just starting out in Waco, Texas, I had no doubts. I thought the death penalty barbaric. Once, in court, I concealed a stiletto in my coat pocket. I walked over to the jury box and said, "If you're going to send this man to the electric chair, you might as well just walk right over there and stab him."

I whipped out the stiletto and tried to hand it to one of the jurors. He cringed, afraid to touch it. For an instant, I thought he was going to faint.

By 1929 I was three years into a busy and, to me, exciting practice. I earned some of my first fees defending the old moonshiners from the rural towns around Waco. Such cases sharpened one's skills at cross and recross.

One morning, in the spring of that year, I was in Tom Scott's office, dividing the cases we had to try in the weeks ahead. Our secretary burst into the room to tell us about a murder.

Over near Moody, at Blue Cut, on the so-called Home place, the bodies of a young white couple had been discovered. Mamie Pedigo was found first, her feet blocking the front screen door, a bullet between the eyes. Her husband, Robert, was sprawled out back by the chopping block, beside his lantern, shot twice, once in the head. A six-year-old son had been spending the night with his grandparents, several miles away. Their little girl, three, was wandering around the small tenant farmhouse, unharmed, but in a daze.

Whenever he heard sensational news, Tom would put on his hat and walk around the block to pick up talk in the street. That day he came back after an hour, worried because feeling was beginning to run high. Groups of men were gathering in the square, on street corners, in cafes and barbershops. Some of the talk was loud and threatening. A lynching had scarred Waco a few years earlier. We both hoped there would not be another.

Waco had two newspapers, the morning *News-Tribune* and the evening *Times-Herald*, owned by the same publisher. For the next three days, the front page of every edition of both papers told of the intensive search for the slayer. Within the week, a suspect, Jordan Scott, the tenant farmer on the place across the Santa Fe tracks, was arrested. The next morning's paper carried a screaming headline: "NEGRO CONFESSES TO PEDIGO MURDERS." The story said that Scott had signed a confession, with his mark, saying that two days before the murder Robert Pedigo had refused to let him come on the property to drink at the water well. He had taken the police to one of the new rows he'd plowed and there, with his pitchfork, had dug up a Winchester .32-20.

The grand jury was in session. It promptly returned indictments charging Jordan Scott with the murder of Mr. and Mrs. Robert Pedigo.

The next day, in the middle of the afternoon, a telephone call summoned me to the chambers of Judge Richard Munroe. He wanted to see me at once. Judge Munroe was plain-spoken, at times even gruff, a venerable jurist with a keen sense of justice and unwavering courage. He presided over the Criminal District Court of McLennan County.

His first words were, "Sit down, son," which I knew meant the discussion would be informal. He had known me since I was a child, and as a young lawyer I had already tried a number of cases in his court.

Now his voice was solemn. "I assume you are keeping up with the accounts of the double slaying at Moody," he began. I nodded. "Jordan Scott," he went on, "is charged with this crime. He is a Negro farm hand who worked the adjoining land. He cannot read or write and has no money to hire a lawyer. He is entitled to a fair trial. To have a fair trial he must have, among other things, legal representation. I have decided to appoint you as his chief counsel, and Sam Darden as your assistant."

The judge paused. "I know the heavy responsibility I am imposing on you. I almost appointed Clay McClellan instead of you." His words struck home. Clay McClellan was middle-aged and successful, a trial lawyer known for his tenacious defenses.

Judge Munroe studied my face as he told me I would have to serve without pay. I would also have to bear any expenses, as the state made no provision for reimbursement. But, he added, as an officer of the court I was obliged to carry out this task to the best of my ability. It was a basic service the legal profession must render—one essential to our judicial process.

He concluded, in measured words, "For reasons you will understand, I must set this case for trial without delay. I am setting it ten days from now and I want you to be ready on that date, if at all possible." This meant dropping everything else and working day and night. But I agreed that any delay in bringing the case to trial would be dangerous. I promised to be ready, if my co-counsel and I humanly could.

Sam Darden was out of town and wouldn't be back until the next morning. Sam was a very able young man. He and I had about the same amount of trial experience and his arguments were noted for their eloquence. I was glad to have him with me.

We were not going to be very popular for the next few weeks. Waco, Texas, was known in 1929, and now, as a church and college town. The home of Baylor University, it is a Baptist citadel, sometimes called "the buckle on the Bible Belt." Waco always wore proudly its label as "A City With a Soul" and boasted of its stately churches, elegant homes, and scenic drives. But in those days a murder case brought out the fear and meanness in any small southern town, especially a murder that was "black on white."

I spent my childhood in Waco, except for a few years when we moved away because of my mother's failing health. My father was a minister, had ridden the circuit on a buckboard, knew everybody. At fifteen I finished high school, then earned my law degrees at Baylor and at George Washington University. I went to court to have my disabilities as a minor removed and was admitted to the State Bar of Texas, at nineteen.

Trial work had been my ambition from my days as a high school debater. I arranged my classes at Baylor Law School so I could spend my spare time in court, watching, listening, learning. To help pay my way, I worked a few hours a day as a secretary in a law office.

Every young attorney interested in trial work should start out with two or three years' experience in the practice of criminal law. Whether you prosecute or defend, you get a faster understanding of human nature and the psychology of a courtroom.

In 1929 I was about to get the kind of experience that lasts a lifetime. When I got to the courthouse, the jailer said he had been expecting me. Word of my appointment had already spread. The jailer, too, had known me most of my life. He led me straight to Jordan Scott's cell and, as he unlocked the solid iron door, called out, "Jordan, here's your lawyer."

The cell resembled the dungeons of old. A few thin rays of light slanted down from a heavily barred window. A small electric bulb hung from the ceiling. Scott sat on the only piece of furniture—a scuffed wooden straight chair. He looked up at me and asked, skeptically, "Is you really a lawyer?"

I told him that the judge had appointed me to defend him, and why. I told him that though I was young (twenty-three), I was not inexperienced. I told him about my co-counsel, Sam Darden.

For half an hour I stressed again and again to Scott the importance of trusting his lawyer and telling him the absolute and complete truth. I hammered home the disastrous results of a client's misleading his lawyer. I assured him that whatever he told me would be kept in complete confidence.

Over and over, Scott said, "God is my witness. I didn't do it. I didn't do it." His voice quivered and his eyes were filled with tears.

"But you're not coming clean," I pressed him. I reminded him of his confession.

"What that?" he asked.

"The confession you signed."

"Didn't sign none. Can't even write."

Then I suggested he must have given the officers one that was written down and read back to him. I said he had probably signed it with an X in the presence of witnesses.

Oh yes, he had done something like that. He said they told him he could either confess, or they would turn him over to a mob. They kept talking about a rope. He said they put their hands on their pistols and threatened him.

"All right, Scott, what did you finally tell them?" I asked.

"I tol' them if they let me go back to my cell and rest, I would tell them I killed those people. I'd been talked to and shouted at and threatened for hours and hours and I was wore out."

I asked what motive he had given for the killings. He said he told the police that the white man had threatened to kill him if he ever came near the well; that he thought he had better get him first; that he sneaked up while the man was cutting wood and shot him. He told them he shot the wife because she was standing in the door and had recognized him.

Then he began to sob. "But I didn't do it, I didn't do it, Mr. . . . . What you say your name was? Oh, believe me, Mr. Judge, I didn't do it."

I had learned before I got to the cell what was in the confession. Step by step, I led him through it. He admitted digging up the gun, his gun. But now he told a story that implicated another fellow, a black named Son Miller, also known as Rockbottom, who had just been released from prison. He and Rockbottom started up the road that night to the Pedigos' house to rob them. Rockbottom talked him into it, he said. But when they got to the bridge over the cut, where the railroad runs along the deep draw, Scott lost heart. Rockbottom called him yellow. Scott gave over the gun and ran back to his house. Later, he heard shots. He hid in the house.

I asked what had happened next. Scott said that after a while Rockbottom appeared. He left the gun and then skipped. When he asked about the shots, Rockbottom said, "Mind your own business." No one had heard of him since. All Scott remembered was that Rockbottom had been in jail in a town near Dallas. Did Son Miller really exist? I thought so.

Painstakingly, I dug into Jordan Scott's past. He had served in the Army in World War I. He thought he was "thirty-seven years old . . . as near as I can come to it." He had been married but did not know where his wife was. He had no children and his parents were dead. He had worked on the farm next to the Pedigos' for only a year. Before that, he picked cotton near Taylor and Pflugerville. He gave the names of the farm owners.

When I knocked on the iron door, the jailer came and unlocked it. As we walked to the outer door, he asked me what I thought about my new case. I said nothing. Before he unlocked the outer door, he gripped my arm tightly and said, "Leon, you better be thinking about pleading this man guilty—and the sooner the better."

Early the next morning I met with Sam Darden and we reviewed what Scott had told me. That afternoon we were on our way to the scene of the murder, interviewing Scott's neighbors, trying to learn all we could about him. People thought well of him. He went to church regularly and did not drink. He was a hard worker, seemed mild-mannered and peaceable.

Next we drove to Taylor and Pflugerville to talk with his former employers. They gave us the finest reports of his industry and behavior. One bachelor farmer, for whom he had worked for several years, said he trusted Jordan Scott completely. He depended on Scott, he said, to look after his unmarried sister and his home when he had to be away, frequently for several days at a time. We asked these people if they would testify for Scott at his trial, and they said they would.

Now we began the search for Rockbottom Miller. All we knew was that he once lived in Dallas and later went to jail in a town not far from there. Beyond that—a blank.

We went back to Scott and told him of our successes and our failures. We questioned him closely, hoping for more leads, but there were none. Before we left, I told Scott that we would probably put him on the witness stand to tell his story—his version of how the confession was obtained, and his account of the meeting with Rockbottom and what the two had done the night of the murders. I told him the district attorney would cross-examine him sharply, to break down his story. It would be an ordeal, I said. Would he, could he, bear up under such an attack? Scott straightened up and, without hesitating, said he could.

I talked to Sam Darden about what legal maneuvers we could try. We could request a change of venue to move the trial to another town. We could ask for a continuance: for more time. What would be gained and what were the risks? A change of venue meant another judge. There was none fairer than Judge Munroe. A change meant jurors of another county—jurors we would not know. Of still graver concern was the possibility that such a motion might stir up a town already restless and trigger a lynch mob. We both knew of cases where this had happened. And if we asked for a continuance, and got it, we ran the same risk.

We decided against filing any motions. We told Scott

his options and reviewed his rights. He agreed with us. We calculated that there was little to be gained by either a postponement or a change of venue—and, conceivably, much to be lost.

Reporters from the newspapers kept after us to find out what Scott's plea would be. We avoided a direct answer, but we were obviously preparing to go to trial. The newspapers predicted a plea of not guilty. Two days before the trial, we told them they were right.

Our course was set. Public opinion had already found Jordan Scott guilty. Who were we to disagree? The threats —and the pressure—began. To complicate matters, I would have to attack the testimony of the sheriff, the constable, the special investigator—people who had known me since I was in swaddling clothes. My poor father had to answer the phone. There were crank calls and anonymous letters, threatening me and my family with bodily harm if I continued to defend Jordan Scott. Some callers demanded that I haul him into court immediately and plead him guilty, notwithstanding his claim of innocence and his legal right to a fair trial.

Some used raw, ugly, menacing words. When my father answered the phone in his study, he heard language not usually spoken to a clergyman. He was not upset by these calls. He felt sorry for those who were ignorant and hated and lacked the courage to say who they were. But I had not expected the calls my partner, Tom Scott, received from people who *did* identify themselves. Two came from clients who threatened to take their business elsewhere if I did not withdraw from the case at once. Three others warned Tom of economic reprisal against our firm. There would be a campaign to induce our clients to find other attorneys.

At my age, at that point in my career, it had not occurred to me that so many people, some of them intelligent, could so misunderstand the law. Didn't they realize what they were saying? A person involved in a popular cause is entitled to good and competent counsel. But a person the public disliked, although his guilt had not been established, should have no counsel. How can a definition of equal justice come from those contradictions?

Some of the sharpest thrusts came from friends I had known since boyhood. Some had been classmates. At first I was heartsick over their taunts and threats. I had never made enemies before. I reminded myself of an old Chinese proverb: "Just as tall trees are known by their shadows, so are good men by their enemies." This was small comfort.

On the morning of the trial, I went to my office early and studied, again, the cases on the admissibility of a confession. I knew that if Scott's confession was admitted in evidence, and the jury believed he made it voluntarily, he would be found guilty and get the death penalty. The trial was to start at 9:30 A.M. I allowed myself twenty minutes to get from my office to the courthouse.

When I arrived, the courtroom was filled to the rafters. There was no more room even to stand. The main aisle leading from the entrance to the front of the courtroom was packed with people. More milled around outside. I could not get in. A deputy sheriff saw my predicament and began to clear a path for me. Inching slowly behind the officer, I heard a husky voice in back of me growl, *"There goes that son of a bitch."* I felt reasonably sure he was not referring to the deputy.

I took my seat at the counsel table and began pulling files and law books out of my briefcase. Sam Darden joined me and soon the side door near the judge's chambers opened. Several officers walked in, then Jordan Scott in handcuffs, and then more officers. A commotion started. Spectators shuffled their feet, almost in rhythm, and there was a buzz of conversation. The sheriff stood on a chair and called for quiet and order. He threatened to clear the courtroom.

Then Judge Munroe walked in, mounted the bench, and turned to the district attorney. He asked for an announcement in the case of *The State of Texas* v. *Jordan Scott*, charging the defendant with the murder of Robert Pedigo. The state had decided to try him on this indictment first.

The district attorney made it clear he would ask for the death penalty. He examined each prospective juror searchingly and carefully to learn whether he had any conscientious scruple against assessing it. When Sam and I examined them, we tried primarily to make sure each juror believed he could give a fair and impartial verdict. We made it clear that we would attack the alleged confession. Jury selection went on the entire day, and until late in the evening. I knew four of the jurors personally. We wound up with the only kind of jury you could get in Texas then: all white, all male.

The newspaper headline the next day said: "MOODY
NEGRO ON TRIAL FOR LIFE; JURY IS SECURED."

It was not until the second day of testimony that the
trial took a dramatic turn. The sheriff and the constable at
Moody described the plowed ground where the gun was
found. Then they reconstructed in detail the circumstances
that led to its discovery. They testified that Scott had taken
them to the spot where the weapon was hidden. This was a
damaging blow, but not unexpected. We had intended for
Scott to tell the story himself when he took the stand: how
Rockbottom had left hurriedly after giving him back the
gun; how he decided to bury the weapon after he saw people gathering at the Pedigo home the next day, knowing
he would be suspected of the crime if it was found in his
possession.

The district attorney then called witnesses who were
present when Scott made his mark at the bottom of the
confession. They testified that he had been warned the
confession could be used against him and that he appeared
to be under no duress. Of course, these witnesses had been
present for only a few minutes and knew nothing about
what had taken place before Scott made his mark. The
prosecution now offered the confession in evidence. We
objected, on the ground that it was not freely and voluntarily made, and asked the court for an opportunity to in-
troduce evidence to support our contention. The court so
ruled.

I called the arresting officers and hammered away at
them, including Constable Duncan, who admitted he was

alone with Scott for "ten or fifteen minutes," and that he "straightened the gun out" but did not cock it.

Q. Well, you placed your hand on the gun and your thumb on the hammer?

A. Well, I guess if something hit the hammer . . . getting it out of my scabbard . . .

Q. Is it necessary to put your thumb on the hammer to straighten out your gun?

A. Not absolutely necessary.

In the end, Judge Munroe ruled that he would leave it to the jury to decide whether the confession was voluntary. If they found otherwise, they were to disregard it.

The confession was then read to the jury. As the district attorney recited the words, in a flat, full voice that rang through the courtroom, I felt that Jordan Scott's fate was sealed. The words were stark:

". . . I had seen Mr. Pedigo out there cutting wood and saw that he had a lantern. . . . I found a kind of little swag in the dump there, a kind of a low place, and I walked up to that and shot Mr. Pedigo. I did not say anything to him, and he did not say anything to me. I do not know where I shot him the first time but he kinda dropped to his knees. Then I shot him again. . . ."

When the district attorney finished, the state rested its case. I announced to the court that Jordan Scott would take the stand. He was emotionless as he went to his seat. He faced the jury. Our questions led him through a brief account of his past. Then I asked, "Did you kill Robert Pedigo?"

"No, sir," he answered emphatically.

"Do you know who killed Robert Pedigo?"

"Son Miller killed him," Scott answered.

He explained that Son Miller was also known as Rock-bottom. He then told the same story he had told me when I first talked with him in the jail. He also testified that while the constable was questioning him, he had talked of using a rope and had threatened to shoot him. An assistant district attorney had cursed and threatened him.

"What, if anything, did the constable say to you about shooting you?" I asked.

"He said if I didn't tell him I did it, he would shoot me, and he pulled his gun out." Scott then added that the constable did not point the gun at him but that he heard a "click-click" down at his side.

"Were you scared?" I asked.

"Sure, I was scared to death."

Several hundred spectators broke into laughter. Sheriff Stegall called for quiet, and Judge Munroe said he would send all those standing out of the courtroom if they did not quiet down.

The district attorney was no slouch at cross-examination. But although Scott was frightened and illiterate, and Dick Holt was skilled and persistent, Scott never faltered.

Q. The very shell that took the life of Mrs. Pedigo was in that gun when you dug it up, wasn't it?

A. I don't know about that.

Q. What did Pedigo say when Son shot him?

A. I didn't hear him. I was running.

Q. Why didn't you run to Son and take the gun?

A. I was afraid he might kill me.

Q. He was your friend, wasn't he?

A. Not all that friend.

Q. Can you tell the jury the name of a single person, white or black, who has seen Son Miller?

A. Won't say that, but Son Miller was the death of those people.

Jordan Scott was one of the best witnesses I ever had. He was uneducated, but cunning. Once, as he addressed the jury, tears streamed down his cheeks. As he left the stand, he dropped to his knees and begged the jurors to believe him.

Although the confession was still a nightmare threat, Scott had set the stage perfectly for the next evidence we had to offer. Our witness was the assistant chief of police of Taylor. "Indeed I know a Son Miller, known as Rockbottom," he testified.)

His words fell like a bombshell on the prosecution. The officer testified that Scott and Miller were friends and were frequently seen together when both had lived near Taylor. The district attorney squirmed in his chair. Only minutes before, he had brushed aside Scott's story, saying, "We might as well be looking for a ghost." Now his exchange over the "mythical" Rockbottom Miller had been flung back at him. To his continued discomfort, the next witness, a farmer, supported the testimony of the Taylor lawman, and described Miller's appearance in virtually the same words as Scott had used.

After calling on the landowners who knew and employed him, as character witnesses, we rested our case. Final arguments were to be heard the next morning.

I opened for the defense and Sam followed, with a memorable speech that never mentioned Jordan Scott but made many affectionate references to Sam's old Negro mammy. Both of us exhorted the jury to disregard the confession because of the manner in which it had been obtained. When we finished, the reaction of the jurors did not inspire us with hope. They seemed noticeably stern.

The district attorney went all out for the death penalty. He worked himself up to a fever pitch. During his plea he pointed to Scott and said, "This colored Negro, this brute, this assassin." We immediately called for a mistrial, arguing that the statement was incurably prejudicial and inflammatory. Even an instruction by the court to the jury to disregard that characterization would not remove the harm that had been done.

The jury deliberated less than an hour before finding Jordan Scott guilty and assessing the sentence at death. Even so, it had stayed out longer than almost everyone in the courtroom expected. We learned later that one of the jurors hesitated to convict in light of the testimony attacking the confession.

Sam and I reflected. We had a condemned man on our hands who still protested he was innocent. Rockbottom Miller was at large. The district attorney chose to ignore him, and the defense had been unable to find him. We decided two things had to be done. First we had to move for a new trial; then we had to locate Rockbottom Miller. Our motion had to be filed quickly.

There were few spectators in the courtroom when our motion was heard. But those who were in the gallery were stunned when Judge Munroe announced he was granting a new trial. He sharply rebuked the district attorney for attempting "to instill in the jury's mind race prejudice."

"NEW TRIAL GRANTED IN MOODY MURDER," was the bold headline of the afternoon paper.

Finally, late on a Saturday afternoon, I learned that Son Miller had been seen in Waxahachie—the town Jordan Scott had in mind when he spoke of a place near Dallas. I decided to get a warrant for his arrest, charging him with the murder of the Pedigos. This was a bold move, but not quixotic. I made the decision only after much deliberation. A client's life was at stake. The sheriff and district attorney had refused to act. Rockbottom was a bird of passage, and to try to question him without arresting him probably would cause him to vanish for good.

I had to move without delay. Sam was out of town, so I went ahead on my own. I called a justice of the peace, a friend, and asked him to meet me at his office. I told him that I wanted a warrant for the arrest of Rockbottom Miller. He begged off. The sheriff and district attorney would resent it; since he operated on the fee system he depended on their good will. I was perplexed. I asked the J.P. if he would come to Judge Munroe's home with me to discuss the matter. He agreed.

Judge Munroe was a charming host, a widower who

loved to have friends call. When we arrived, he showed no immediate interest in our problem. He was more concerned with being hospitable. I finally broached the subject of bringing Rockbottom Miller to Waco for an examining trial. Since I could not get the officers to question him, this was my only alternative. The justice of the peace then explained his predicament. Judge Munroe did not hesitate. "Issue the warrant," he growled. "Neither the sheriff nor the district attorney has any right to run your court."

Early the next morning I was on my way to Waxahachie. There I went directly to the office of the jailer to look at his records. I was stunned to find that, on the day before the murder of the Pedigos, Son Miller had been released from the county jail, so the records bore out what Jordan Scott had told me. He had served a sentence for gaming. Of even more significance, the jailer told me that when Rockbottom was released he had said he was "headed for Waco."

I found Miller and had the warrant served on him. I returned to Waco in my car, alone, excited over what I had learned and oblivious to anything except the thought of whether Rockbottom was really involved in the murder.

The arrival of the officers from Waxahachie with their prisoner caused a flurry of commotion in the McLennan County Courthouse. The newspaper reporters had a field day. As Rockbottom was led from the police car to the jail, a crowd of curious onlookers gathered. Jordan Scott heard the noise. He peered through a slit in the bars of his cell, just in time to see Rockbottom pass below his window.

Both had words to say about who was "setting in jail now," and who was going to be setting in there still or soon.

The examining trial settled that question. Son Miller had an absolute, ironclad alibi. Although he had gone to Waco after his release from jail, he did not leave Waxahachie until two days after the murders. Three witnesses testified that he was in Waxahachie on the night of the murders.

I felt so badly about Miller's unjust confinement, and the inconvenience he suffered, that I gave him thirty-five dollars of my own money—a sum not easily come by in those days. It was to pay him for the time he lost and to provide travel money. I tried to explain that his arrest was all part of my duty to defend Scott as best I could. But this did not make me feel much better.

My next move was instinctive. I went straight to the cell of Jordan Scott. I had spent weeks convincing myself that my client might just barely be innocent. Now I demanded the truth. I told him I had fought for his life with every ounce of energy and effort I could gather. I reminded him that I had begged him to tell me the full story, so I could do my best for him. But no, I continued, he had deceived me, had caused me trouble, cost me money, and no small amount of distress. Now I knew that Rockbottom had nothing to do with the murders. "Are you going to tell me the truth," I asked, "or keep leading me up a blind alley?"

Scott said he was sorry for the trouble he had caused, but he stuck to his story. I looked at him and said nothing. "What are you going to do now?" he asked, nervously.

"I don't know," I said. I moved toward the cell door. One rap would bring the jailer to let me out.

"Don't leave," he pleaded. Then came a long pause. "Mr. Jaworski, if I tell you the whole truth, will you try to save me from that chair?"

I said I would, by every legal means.

Then the story tumbled out. Yes, he had killed the Pedigos. But the confession the law forced out of him told less than the full story. It did not tell of Pedigo's threat, after Scott stopped in his tracks. The farmer had shouted, "If I ever see you over here again, I'll kill you." And Scott had called back, "Suppose I get you first?"

That evening he went home, still brooding over their clash. "The more I thought about it, the more worried I got; and the more I worried, the more scared I got. Finally I took my gun, started for his place, and you know the rest."

I asked about Mrs. Pedigo. He lowered his head. I could hardly hear him when he said that he knew she could identify him. "I know you," she had cried out, "you're the one who had the row with my husband." He lost his head and killed her.

Neither of us spoke for a few moments. Scott broke the silence. He looked up and asked, "Is you going to quit me now?"

"No," I said. "I should but I won't. Besides, I made you a promise and I'll try to keep it."

I was not prepared for what happened next. Scott moved slowly toward me. I could see in his face the fear that I might abandon or, worse, betray him. I had only a split sec-

ond in which to act. I happened to be near an old, upright
bathtub in the corner of his cell. One of the iron legs
was wobbly. Quickly I reached down and pulled it loose
from the tub. I held him off with that makeshift club,
backed myself against the solid iron door, and banged away
until the guard arrived and got me out of there.

When I returned to my office, I found it difficult to
think clearly. For weeks we had been fighting for a man's
life, when his guilt was in some doubt. I was to defend him
again soon, but now I knew him to be guilty. I shuddered
at the memory of the two dead people, so young, and the
two little orphans. The overwhelming weight of public
opinion had tried to crush me because it said Jordan Scott
was guilty and I said he was not. Now I knew the rest were
right and I was wrong.

Early the next morning, I met Sam Darden and told him
what had happened. Together we went to see Jordan Scott.
He knew I was going to stand by him now. He was calm,
to the point of being numb. He paid little attention when
we told him his trial had been set in one week. We prod-
ded until he turned to me and said he had spent the night
regretting what he had told me. Not until we reassured
him that we would continue our efforts to save him from
the electric chair did he finally show any spirit.

I told Scott to listen carefully. What I had to say was extremely important. There could be no more talk about
Rockbottom Miller in the second trial. We would question
the officers, just as before, to try to establish that his confession was forced. But—and this I stressed—we could not
put him on the witness stand. A lawyer cannot place a wit-

ness on the stand to swear to falsehoods, I explained. If we allowed him to repeat the Rockbottom story, that would mean that we as lawyers had knowingly let him swear to a lie.

Jordan stared at me, unbelieving. I told him that if he was determined to stand by the Rockbottom Miller story, we had no choice but to ask the court to appoint other attorneys to defend him. He said he didn't want other attorneys. He was satisfied with us.

"Jordan," Sam Darden asked, "have you given any thought to pleading guilty and asking for mercy?"

He shook his head. "No, suh. Never. They'd burn me for sure. Look at the fight you put up the first time, and still they give me the chair."

There was another silence.

Scott's eyes searched the floor. Looking up, he admitted that he knew he could never get away with the Rockbottom story. He said he guessed the best thing for him to do was just keep his mouth shut. I told him that, under our system of law, he was entitled to say nothing. The state could not call him to the stand. The district attorney could not even refer to his silence in his argument to the jury. What he had told us, I added, was known in law as a privileged communication between a lawyer and his client. We could not reveal it, and no one could make us reveal it.

"All I want now," he said, "is to be saved from that chair. But if you do all you can, and the law says I got to die for what I done, I will be ready to go. I know what I done was wrong."

As we left the jail, Darden clutched my elbow and said,

"Leon, as far as I'm concerned, I'm going to fight like hell to save his life. He made a mistake. He killed when he was scared—lost his mental balance."

I admired Sam for his determination, but I wondered whether he was kidding himself, even as I had, into believing that there was any hope of saving Jordan Scott from paying with his life. As we talked, Sam turned every aspect of the case over and over in his mind. What finally came out was that he opposed capital punishment—at least in this case. There was no reason, he said, to execute an illiterate pauper because he had lost his senses. I had scant hope that Sam would succeed in saving Scott with this argument, but I admired him for trying and told him so.

By the time of the second trial, even the curious had lost interest. On the first day the courtroom was half empty. But by the time the final arguments began, the seats were almost filled. Again, I opened for the defense. Sam followed. He was at his best. He launched a terrific attack on capital punishment, pacing up and down in front of the jury box. He whispered. He shouted. He waved his arms and stamped his feet. As serious as the matter was, there occurred one comic moment.

At one point, Sam, to emphasize his argument, drew back with his right arm, his hand clenched in a fist, and swung it in front of him—a roundhouse swing. A juror who had been leaning back in his chair tilted forward at about the time Sam's fist flashed in an arc, missing the man's chin by a whisker. The startled juror jerked back. Even Judge Munroe laughed.

The district attorney was more restrained in his closing

argument than at the first trial. He was not about to risk another judicial rebuke. Repeatedly he asked the jury either to bring in the death penalty or to acquit the defendant. He argued, as prosecutors often do, that there was no middle ground.

In less than thirty minutes, the jury found Jordan Scott guilty and fixed his punishment as death in the electric chair.

We filed a motion for a new trial, and were overruled. We carried the case to the Court of Criminal Appeals, and lost. We had reached the end of the line. In 1929 the United States Supreme Court was not accepting jurisdiction in cases of this nature.

In the meantime, with some misgivings, I had accepted a position with the Houston law firm of A. D. Dyess. By Labor Day I had moved to Houston. Jordan Scott was on death row at the state penitentiary in Huntsville. The first Saturday I could, I went to see him.

The warden asked me if I planned to plead insanity on Scott's behalf. The question startled me. I said no. He said, "Don't be too sure."

I did not recognize Jordan Scott. He had not eaten for days or spoken to anyone for a month. He was lying on the concrete floor completely nude, twitching at times. I saw a creature of skin and bones. The warden left us alone and I tried to talk to Scott. He either did not understand, or else chose to ignore me. His execution was two days away, on Monday.

Later, I stepped across the street to a pay telephone and called Governor Dan Moody in Austin. I told him what I had seen. I suggested that Jordan Scott might be insane and that he should be examined immediately. The governor was irritated that the matter had not been called to his attention until almost the eve of execution. I explained that I had just become aware of the facts.

I drove back to Houston. On Monday morning I received a telegram from Governor Moody, advising me that the prison doctor had found Jordan Scott to be sane. I felt sick—as we say in Texas, *blue* sick. But I returned to Huntsville immediately and asked permission of the warden to be alone with Scott for an hour or two.

He was on the floor, as he had been. I leaned over and begged him to talk. Finally, he stirred. I raised his head and placed a pillow under it. Leaning directly over him, I spoke slowly and distinctly: "Jordan, Mr. Darden and I have done all we can for you. It has been ordered that you must die. Do you remember our conversation in your cell in Waco? You said, 'If the law believes I should die for what I've done, I will be ready to go.' Now I want you to do just that. There are only a few hours left to get ready to go."

The first indication I had that Scott recognized me, and understood what I was saying, was when tears began rolling down his face. But he said nothing for fifteen or twenty minutes.

I started to leave. "Just a minute," he said, feebly. "Wait—just a minute longer, please."

He appeared to be gathering his strength. I waited. A half-smile replaced the vacant stare on his face. "Thanks for everything," he said. "But would you do one more thing for me?"

"I will if I can, Jordan."

"Tell Judge Munroe I thank him for being so fair to me. Then tell him the true story—what I told you that night in Waco. Will you?" These words came haltingly, for he was so weak he could hardly talk.

I said I would, and I asked him to do something for me: see the prison chaplain. He nodded, and we said our good-bys.

I went to the warden's office; I told him Scott was talking and wanted the prison chaplain to visit him. The warden said the chaplain had tried to help before, and failed. Scott wouldn't see him. "I think he will now," I said.

As I drove home, my thoughts were completely absorbed in the fate of Jordan Scott. I was in Houston before I realized it. In the morning paper I read about his execution. The chaplain walked at his side, saying a prayer. When they strapped him in the chair, he straightened right up. His last words were, "Lord, have mercy on my soul."

I thought about the death penalty most of that day, and many times in the years since. When I was young, and filled with doubts, I read all I could find by and about Clarence Darrow and Robert Ingersoll. Neither believed in God. Darrow, in fact, believed in very little. Ingersoll was this nation's greatest orator of the nineteenth century, a lawyer with a poetic command of language. Both fiercely opposed the death penalty, and their writings influenced me greatly.

If anyone ever deserved capital punishment, it was Jordan Scott. I had grown close to him and had tried to save his life. But here was a fellow who had killed a man in a sneak shooting, then murdered his wife in cold blood.

What I have finally come to in my own mind is a compromise. I believe the death penalty should apply in the case of a man who kills a law officer in the routine conduct of his duties, of a convict who kills attempting to escape, in the slaying of any hostage.

The death penalty is still under review in Texas, as in other states. I am not sure that it deters crime. As a general rule, I believe the death penalty should be avoided. I take that stand, not on religious grounds, but simply in the conviction that if we err, it must be on the side of the innocent man wrongly condemned.

Jordan Scott was the first and only client I ever lost to the electric chair. A few days after his execution, I received a letter from the only black lawyer practicing in Waco at the time. He wrote to tell me that Jordan Scott had an insurance policy with the Veterans Administration from his service in World War I. After deducting what he had borrowed, and the unpaid premiums, there was maybe $200 left. He had asked that it be paid over to me. I deducted some expenses and turned the rest over to charity. I was touched deeply by the gesture, by Jordan Scott's sense of obligation. Of course, I was glad I had not known earlier that I had a beneficial interest in the death of my client.

3

Rich Man

Houston in the 1930s was what one writer would later describe as a whiskey and trombone town. The city was short on culture, but long on credit and faith and ambition.

Streetcar tracks ran through cobbled streets, and large magnolia trees shaded the antebellum homes on Montrose and Heights boulevards. The *old* money had been made in land and cattle and cotton, by families who had come to Texas in the days of Stephen F. Austin and Sam Houston. The great oil fortunes were creating a generation of the new rich and changing the city's texture.

Whatever social life Houston offered then, I had no entree to it and little time for it. I was starting both a career and a family. In 1931, a month after I joined Fulbright, Crooker, I married Jeannette Adam, a brunette as pretty as Waco could grow them. Ours had not been a fast courtship. We had known each other since grade school. Jean-

nette later played the organ in my father's church and I
would sit there, in my only suit, and sneak glances at her.
In Houston, in the mid-1930s, our three children were
born: Joan, Claire, and Joseph.

It was not a generous time to be raising a family. The
country had slid deeper into the depression. Though
affected less than most cities, Houston had its soup kitch-
ens. The unemployed lined up for blocks to receive the soup
dished out by the churches and the Salvation Army.

An average salary for a secretary or an office worker was
$10 to $12 a week. Store clerks worked for less and felt
lucky to have a job. A new Ford or Chevrolet cost about
$700. Bread was a nickel a loaf, eggs cost eight cents a
dozen, and Hanes shorts sold four to a dollar.

I rode the bus to work. Some days I did not see the sun.
I left in the dark of morning, with the babies stirring, and
returned at night. I couldn't wait to get to the office. I was
doing what I most wanted, trying lawsuits, one right after
another, all kinds. In 1935, at the age of twenty-nine, I became the firm's youngest partner.

By now my clients were no longer moonshiners or indi-
gents accused of murder. They were some of the city's
major firms, and older families, and the young, hard
chargers coming up behind them, mostly lone wolves,
going for broke. One was a self-made oilman named Glenn
McCarthy.

At least once in his career, every attorney should have a
client such as Glenn McCarthy, if only to remind us that
the practice of law treats not with the abstract but with
people—their hearts and tempers.

McCarthy may have been the most colorful figure I ever represented. He was the prototypical Texas wildcatter, the model for Jett Rink in Edna Ferber's monolithic novel *Giant*, the character played on the screen by James Dean. Glenn was self-made, moody, audacious, hard-eyed, and big-fisted, a football tramp who once played for a college and high school team in the same season. He married Faustine Lee, a sweetheart of his school days and the daughter of a millionaire Houston oilman, whose dollars could have been of great help to Glenn, had he wanted them. Which he did not. McCarthy was determined to make his fortune on his own. And he did. He lost it the same way.

It is altogether too slick, too simple, to say that he was a throwback to a more romantic age, an America that once was and can never be again. But, with his dark, flinty looks and trim mustache, he had the air and instincts of a Mississippi riverboat gambler.

By the early 1950s McCarthy had emerged as a full-blown Texas legend. He was a man who challenged the establishment, in the days when few people knew who or what the establishment was. When Glenn built the Shamrock Hotel in 1949, his achievement went beyond money, luxury, or property. The Shamrock was the first major hotel in Houston to be owned by anyone other than Jesse Jones, the financier and former commerce secretary under Franklin Roosevelt.

One man cannot build a city, but one man can be the catalyst. In Houston, Jesse Jones was that man. He owned the biggest bank, the leading newspaper, and the most hotels, and people once said that a marble could roll for miles

in Houston without leaving land owned by Jesse Jones.
During the war, as Secretary of Commerce, he oversaw the
Reconstruction Finance Corporation, which made loans to
little men and great nations. It was Jones who said, "Britain is a good risk for a loan." The line now must seem a
droll understatement, but in truth it reassured our country,
and theirs, at a time when German planes were pounding
British soil nightly.

In the 1930s and 1940s little of importance happened in
Houston without the approval of Jesse Jones, or against his
wishes. But Jones admired Glenn McCarthy as another
self-made man, and though I can't say that he offered him
credit or even influence, he did nothing to hold Glenn
back. Texans who play for high stakes are not so eager to
have help as they are not to have opposition. They are like
the character in a song made famous by Phil Harris, who
found himself confronting a bear and uttered a simple
prayer: "Lord, if you can't help me, please don't help that
bear."

McCarthy was the kind of man who would consider a
request for help an act of weakness. He was the host, never
the guest. When he opened the Shamrock Hotel, on Saint
Patrick's Day of 1949, thousands of celebrities arrived from
all over the country. He had 2,500 shamrocks flown in
from Ireland. At the top of his game, he bought a radio station, a chemical plant, a fifteen-thousand-acre ranch, and a
men's clothing store. He bought a nursery and used its
stock to landscape the lawns of his mansion, then sold the
company for a profit. People spoke of him as The

McCarthy, as though the name were a Middle Eastern
title.

But always, in good times or lean, he was a lightning rod
for those looking for trouble or fast bucks. As it turned out,
I was Glenn's trial lawyer in some of the most unusual
cases an advocate could ever expect to encounter.

Our association began around 1936, when Glenn was
drilling for oil at Conroe, in a field some thirty miles north
of Houston. He had leased the drilling equipment, was operating on a very thin budget, and was behind in his payments to the rig owners as well as to his crew. All of which
was fairly standard among that breed of men who called
themselves wildcatters. Their edge was their nerve, their
ability to talk investors and suppliers out of their money
and equipment in return for a cut of future profits.

The wildcatter had to be a gambler, a trader, and an entrepreneur. He existed for the purpose of finding new de-
posits of oil, or digging deeper in fields the major companies had abandoned. The majors could drill anywhere,
and turn up endless dry holes without making a dent in
their budgets. The wildcatter put his neck on the line every
day.

The wildcatters were to their era what the old gold
miners had been to theirs a hundred years earlier. But
sadly, the era is gone. There is little place left for the wildcatters in today's financially sophisticated, high-technology
petroleum industry. Soaring costs, tight money, oil price
ceilings, and a reduced oil depletion allowance have all
conspired to thin their ranks. Most of those who survive
now are college-trained, in geology and economy, who take

their chances on offshore or overseas exploration. The wildcatters today are the money manipulators.

No one can operate now the way McCarthy once did. At
Conroe, when I first encountered Glenn, he was keeping
his men on the job partly because they believed in him,
and partly because he threatened to whip anyone who tried
to leave.

But the owners of the drilling equipment were not so
easily pacified. They were nervous over the possible damage
to their rig, as well as with a reasonable fear that the rental
would not be paid soon—if at all. The owners obtained an
injunction in Montgomery County to restrain Glenn from
further use of the equipment until the past due rental was
paid and steps were taken to protect the equipment from
continuing damage.

McCarthy was at a critical point in his operation—he
was about to drill the plug—and in his frame of mind was
not about to concern himself with the judge's injunction.
For days his crew had screened him from the local sheriff,
but the papers were finally served.

One of McCarthy's investors in the well was M. D. Anderson, of Anderson, Clayton and Company, then the largest cotton traders in the world. Anderson was about seventy, a generous and sensitive man whose estate would
endow the foundation that bears his name, one that would
make Houston a center for cancer research. It was Anderson's habit, as well as his pleasure, to watch the drilling
from the rear seat of his Cadillac. But each day he grew
more worried. He was an astute businessman. He knew
that the restraining order signed by the judge, and served

on Glenn as Anderson looked on, was not to be taken lightly. He had his chauffeur drive him into town so that he could telephone his close friend, and my law partner, Colonel William B. Bates.

Anderson described the situation to Bates, who in turn asked me to drive to Conroe and take such steps as were necessary to turn aside the injunction. I was thirty, not all that familiar with the oil business or the driven men whose life it was.

The drilling site, in the thick of the pinewoods common to that area, was not easy to find. When I located it, I found the old gentleman in his usual spot in the rear of the Cadillac. He was ashen-faced, visibly shaken, and sputtering disjointed sentences, from which I gathered he had just witnessed some horrifying spectacle. Finally I was able to piece together what had taken place, an incident he kept referring to as a "miracle." Only moments before, a platform some fifty feet above the ground had collapsed as Glenn, his brother, Bill, and another worker were standing on it. As the three men were falling, Glenn had grabbed a cross-iron, and the other two grabbed him. His brother clung to Glenn's waist and the third man to his leg.

"Glenn not only held himself and the two others securely," Mr. Anderson said, sputtering, "he then maneuvered the lowering of all three to the ground." McCarthy had suffered friction burns on both hands, sliding down the derrick to safety. Otherwise they were all uninjured.

Toiling in the oilfields had made McCarthy strong. But M. D. Anderson's description of the event had the ring of fiction woven with fact. As I began to question his story,

McCarthy walked up, stoic, unexcited, and austere. He looked a little like Barrymore's Hamlet. When Anderson introduced us, Glenn merely grunted. He made no reference whatever to his acrobatic landing and his manner discouraged any questions. But those involved, and the others who witnessed it, repeated the story until it became a part of McCarthy lore.

He joined us in the car and I tried to explain the penalties for violating an injunction. Glenn looked at me and said nothing. He was one of those people who, early in life, had mastered the art of using silence as a weapon. Finally I turned to Anderson, who nodded and told me, yes, to proceed to dissolve the injunction. A compromise had to be worked out with the plaintiffs. In such matters a lawyer is guided by one basic question: What is the most I can obtain for my client, and the least that can be given away? To finish the job, Glenn needed time and freedom. Anderson was willing to advance an additional sum of money to provide them.

I drove into Conroe, called on my adversaries in their offices, and then worked with them until past midnight before we came to terms I thought I could justify. Then I sat down at the secretary's desk and typed the agreement. It was not a masterpiece of typing, but it reflected the terms. At two in the morning we signed the agreement and, wearily, I sent word to Anderson that all was well. The injunction would be dismissed as soon as the judge arrived in court. Glenn did strike oil, and his investors and his creditors were repaid.

Years later, after I had represented McCarthy in a num-

ber of other actions, he and I were visiting in his office at
the Shamrock. By then the hotel was accepted as a national showplace, although Frank Lloyd Wright had described its architecture as "tragic." We were speaking nos-
talgically of the earlier days when I said, "Glenn, do you
remember when we first met at the drilling site near
Conroe?"

He responded instantly, "Oh yes, I'll never forget it."

I laughed and said, "Glenn, I might as well admit to
you, on that particular occasion I thought you were about
the most boorish client I ever tried to serve."

McCarthy stared at me for a few seconds and then said,
"I guess we're even, then. I thought you were about the
dumbest lawyer I ever met."

The earnest lawyer often enters a case with the zeal of a
missionary. Truth and protection are the fish he peddles.
But McCarthy had been to town, he had worked and
fought with his own hands, had seen the earth's treasures.
He was not all that hot to be protected. He was the kind of
oilman that Hollywood had immortalized in the film
Boom Town, with Clark Gable and Spencer Tracy.

Glenn had been born with the sound of oil rigs in his
ears. His father had been a driller at Spindletop, in the
early years of the great East Texas oil boom. As a boy
Glenn rode to the field with his father in a two-wheeled
horse buggy. One day, during a hurricane, he crouched in
the darkness as the winds toppled derrick after derrick. The
family later moved to Houston and he grew up in the city's
tough, bloody Fifth Ward, where, he once said, "The cops

were afraid of the people, and there was almost always a
dead man somewhere on the street in the morning."

I don't know that I have ever known a more stubborn or
determined man. To earn enough of a stake to permit him
to drill for oil, he pressed pants, drove rivets, owned and
ran two gas stations. He lost everything he had drilling
three dry holes. On the third, in Hardin County, he
drafted his father as a tool pusher, and dug six thousand
feet with a leaking, secondhand boiler and a "coffeepot" rig
that broke down endlessly. Sand ruined the rubber rings in
his pumps every half hour. It was agonizing toil and, after
six months, he came up empty. "We might as well have
been drilling with a high-heeled boot," said Glenn, in his
own blunt way. Modern equipment would have drilled
that hole in a week.

But Glenn would not quit, he never has, and at Conroe
his first well came in. Then he struck it big in Chambers
County, and one day the Humble Oil Company sent him a
check for $700,000 for his leases. He was twenty-six. He
bought a big diamond ring and built a mansion.

The next time I heard from him, he looked the part of
the successful wildcatter. He had the diamond ring and his
clothes had the stamp of custom tailoring. He reeked of
confidence. But he still had little taste for social pleasant-
ries. He got straight to the point. An oil company in Oklahoma was suing Glenn for a substantial amount of money,
based on an alleged breach of contract in connection with
a well he was drilling for them.

He asked me to represent him and I agreed. We decided
to file a countersuit for the remainder due him under the

contract. At stake was not only a large amount of cash, but
the "reasonable value" of lease acreage that was to be assigned to him as the drilling progressed. As long as the well
was being drilled, and no adverse showings were encountered, this acreage had a market value. The oil company
withheld it at a time when Glenn could have sold out for
considerable profits.

McCarthy had begun to drill the latter stages of the well
under difficult conditions. Most of his crew received their
wages late and a number fell out with him. The oil company eventually seized on this disenchantment and undertook to use these crew members as helpful witnesses.

When I learned of this development, it occurred to me
that no time should be lost in committing all potential
witnesses to their knowledge of the facts. Paul Strong, an
able trial lawyer, was then working with me. Paul set out to
conduct the interviews, obtaining affidavits from each
member of the crew regarding the manner in which the
well was drilled—to what depths, under what practices.
The oil company had indicated that it would contend that
the depth claimed by McCarthy had never been reached,
and that the well was drilled in a manner that varied from
the permissible angles. Other claims amounting to fraud
were asserted, as well.

The affidavits Paul Strong obtained contradicted these
claims, and we prepared for trial. When Glenn arrived at
the courthouse he was sporting his flashy diamond and was
dressed in clothes a wealthy man might wear to his daughter's wedding. Patiently, I asked him to remove his ring, return home, and put on a more dignified and businesslike

attire. He gave me a look that would exterminate head lice.
But Glenn was a good soldier and he did as I requested. I
cautioned him about the possible reaction of jurors to a
witness whose manner seems cocky and arrogant.

During the trial, Glenn was subjected to a rigid cross-examination on the charges by the oil company. He made a
fine, forthright witness. He answered all questions directly
and without the slightest evasion.

When the lawyers for the oil company presented their
witnesses, we saw a parade of men who had been members
of Glenn's crew. They took the witness stand one by one to
support the oil company's charges that the hole marked by
McCarthy was never drilled and the other provisions of the
contract were not observed.

But we were armed with the affidavits my associate had
taken and, one by one, these witnesses were knocked off
and their credibility destroyed. The situation became almost comic. On cross-examination, I began to inquire
where these witnesses had been staying and what they had
been doing since their arrival in Houston to testify in the
case. It developed that they had been wined and dined,
lavishly entertained, by the oil company. It did not take
the jury very long to catch on that their testimony was
prejudiced. When the verdict was returned, McCarthy received all of the money for which he had sued, as well as
damages representing the value of the leases that had been
withheld.

McCarthy was a feast-or-famine character. Once he developed a field in West Beaumont that had a tremendous
gas reserve. One of the wells was particularly difficult to

control, and great quantities of mud had to be pumped in to keep the gas from causing the well to blow. Despite these efforts, the well blew out one night, sending about one hundred twenty feet of drill stem whistling through the air, then catching on fire, melting the derrick to the ground, and raging uncontrollably for a number of days. The losses were estimated at a quarter of a million dollars.

Finally the blowout was brought under control. The winds, however, had caused the salt water to spew over rice fields some distance away, and a layer of oil and muck covered the adjoining land. The landowners and rice growers brought suit against McCarthy, claiming that the well had been negligently drilled and that McCarthy was responsible for the damage they had suffered.

Glenn asked me to take the case. He was totally without insurance. Nor did the evidence seem to weigh in his favor. Glenn did not seem to get himself into those simple multimillion-dollar antitrust actions that many lawyers crave.

I soon learned that the driller who had been on the night shift when the blowout occurred had turned against McCarthy. As a witness for the other side, his testimony could have been devastating to our defense. He claimed that he had warned McCarthy that the well was "bucking," and that more mud should be pumped into the hole. He said McCarthy disagreed, subjected him to profanity, and threatened to fire him if he did not follow orders. The driller also contended that McCarthy's methods were unacceptable in the drilling business. The jury was composed almost entirely of refinery workers. To them such a charge was bound to be taken as negligence.

McCarthy assured me that the accusations were nothing but bull's wool, and that the driller was trying to smear him. I needed to see how far the man would go under oath, and I moved to take his oral deposition. When I arrived at the courthouse the driller was waiting, slouched in a chair, with the attorneys for the plaintiffs beside him. I was deliberately carping and baiting as I examined him. He clearly resented some of my questions and some of my intimations, and a little arrogance began to surface. Whereupon I grilled him even more closely and sharply, implying all along that he had been lying.

After two hours the deposition ended. As I was closing my briefcase, the driller rose out of his chair and glared at me. At that moment he seemed to be nearly seven feet tall; certainly he was a much more imposing man than I had judged him to be while I was examining him. As I left the building, I wondered if I would have been quite so abrasive in my questioning had I seen the witness standing first.

I now began to plan our strategy for the trial. I wanted to have as much time elapse as possible, in order to give the land an opportunity to restore itself. I had hoped that through rains, and nature's own cycle, the land, now almost bald, would improve. We had taken a soil analysis and found a heavy salt content. I obtained one continuance, and the judge sent word to me that the case would be set for trial in the spring, with no further postponements to be granted.

A week before the trial I visited the blighted fields. Much to my surprise, there were green sprigs of grass all over the land and trees we had thought dead were leafing.

The warm days were helping the growth of new foliage. When I saw the sprigs of grass I arranged to have some cattle brought in from a neighboring farm, and they found this young grass much to their liking. I then sent for a photographer skilled in the use of colored movies, which were an innovation at the time. We took considerable footage of the cows eating the grass, and arty shots of the leafing trees framed against the midday sun.

I shipped the film to St. Louis to be developed. At the time, it was the nearest city where this process could be done quickly. When the film was returned, I found the pictures clear and revealing.

When the trial began, one of the landowners described the plight that had befallen his fields. On cross-examination, I asked him when he last visited the land, and he said that he had been there "only yesterday." I asked if he saw any signs of life and he said none whatever. I asked about the sprigs of grass and he laughed at the thought. I asked about the leafing trees and he responded that there was not a single sign of life on the place.

Then I began to summarize his testimony, describing the land as worthless—as devoid of any life as the Sahara Desert. I carried him to the full length of his insistence that the land was hopeless from the standpoint of production.

After the plaintiffs rested their case, I asked the judge to have the courtroom darkened, so that I might present some movies. This proposal brought on strong objections from the plaintiffs, not unexpectedly. We spent an entire day arguing the admissibility of these movies, inasmuch as there was no precedent in Texas for such a presentation. I placed on the stand my photographer, who testified that the films portrayed accurately the actual scene. I then contended that the films were just as admissible as a photograph would be, once the proper predicate of accuracy had been laid. I *had* to get the films into evidence. Without them my defense was far less dramatic.

At the end of the argument, the court ruled that the films would be admitted. The courtroom was darkened, and when the jurors saw the scenes of the cows munching the grass and the trees leafing, it was obvious that the plaintiffs had lost their case. The jury returned a verdict of no negligence on McCarthy's part and found that the land had not been damaged.

Glenn McCarthy was one of those people who are vulnerable to lawsuits. The rich, the famous, the controversial often are. I have sometimes felt that severe penalties should be imposed for suits found to be clearly frivolous. Of course, some would argue that the legal fees are punishment enough, but this is not always so.

No one can be in the oil business very long, or very seriously, without getting involved in a suit over land leases. In some corners of Texas, titles were often clouded and chicanery commonplace. Bitter stories have long been told of men who lost leases in a poker game, or signed them away for almost nothing, and later saw them enrich others. The late H. L. Hunt left behind a long string of old prospectors clinging to such laments.

McCarthy was sued in a land action over leases in the Friendswood area, in what is called a trespass to try title suit. His leases were said to be invalid, another party claimed to own them, and damages were asked. After taking a close look at the records, I could see no merit to the case. But, of course, a lawyer just does not assume that a suit is without merit. There is always the possibility that facts exist, unknown to him, that may well change the complexion of the case.

But I went to trial feeling that the plaintiffs could offer no evidence that would entitle them to go to a jury. The court would simply find that, as a matter of law, they had failed to show an actionable case.

I was right. During the trial, the opposing counsel tried to obscure the fact that he had no evidence by issuing a flurry of subpoenas for witnesses of whom I had never heard. But I still had to be concerned as to what information, if any, the witnesses might have. It was a strange charade. Several took the stand and shed no light whatsoever on the issues involved in the case. They were what theater people call a *divertissement*, a diversion from the plot.

Finally, a subpoena "instanter" was issued. My client was entitled to an instructed verdict if no further proof was offered by the plaintiff. His attorney was now frantically resorting to the subpoena power to bring in a witness he hoped could supply the needed testimony to have the case go to the jury. Naturally, with a win in my bag, I was eagerly hoping that the witness who had been subpoenaed instanter had nothing worthwhile to offer.

This is the essence of the "mystery" witness, that staple of so many film and television dramas, an idea guaranteed to inspire a courtroom buzz and an exchange of nervous glances among opposing counsel. But all too often the witness is to a case what the mask is to a wrestler: an adornment.

The court had declared a recess and the mystery witness was out in the hall, waiting for court to resume and to be called to the stand. As customary with me, I felt it my duty to interrogate the witness to see what information he might have. I did not know the man, but I walked up to him, introduced myself, and began to chat, hoping I would gain some insight into his testimony. Except for telling me his name, he was mute. I made no headway whatever. Finally I said, "Well, I just wanted to visit with you because I had not heard of you before." Quickly he replied, "Well, that makes us even—I hadn't heard of you, either." Thus ended the interview.

No matter. The witness had very little else to say once he took the stand. A short time later, the judge instructed the jury to bring in a verdict in favor of McCarthy.

In those days, McCarthy saw life as a contest, to be won, not by the side with the best lawyers, but by the fellow who was willing to work the hardest and stay the latest. He could go without sleep or food and drink for days, without showing any unsteadiness. Even in his most normal periods, he could awaken, apparently fresh, after a few hours of sleep, toss off a vodka and tomato juice, reread his leases or study his maps, and impatiently await the new dawn.

It wasn't always his oilfield adventures that brought him into court. Sometimes his temper did. One day, in 1950, I received a phone call from A. G. McNeese, then serving as Glenn's top executive assistant as well as his general counsel. Mac said a suit had been filed in the federal court in Los Angles against Glenn, and he hoped I would defend him. I walked over to their offices to hear more about the case. This was what I learned:

In September of 1949 a Hollywood sports promoter, Larry Rummans, had flown to Houston to stage a charity football game for McCarthy. While in town he had lavishly used his host's name and credit. Among other transgressions, he had contacted gamblers in Las Vegas and in Glenn's name wagered $1,500 on Villanova to beat Texas A&M. When McCarthy learned of the bet, through a telephone call that came to him by mistake, he was outraged. Not only had his name been used without his knowledge, but the bet was *against* his old school.

McCarthy was an avid sports fan, who had proposed and designed a covered stadium fifteen years before the Astrodome was erected. He had no objection to gambling on games. But he preferred to do his own. He did not take kindly to impostors.

He summoned the Californian to his office at the Shamrock. After an exchange of words, during which he called Rummans a parasite and a liar, Glenn fired him from any further connection with the charity football promotion. The encounter became more and more heated, until McCarthy delivered his final message, as he sometimes did, with his fist. He then ordered his security officer to hold the fellow in his room at the Shamrock until all of the accounts were in order. He was detained for three days and Glenn released him.

McCarthy knew a suit would be filed, with California

the likely site. His idea of keeping a low profile was to fly to the Rose Bowl game in Pasadena, where he could be served with the papers. The promoter was suing him for $210,000, charging permanent injury to his jaw and back as a result of the attack by McCarthy. He also alleged false imprisonment. Of course, Glenn felt he had let the scoundrel off lightly and the suit was unjustified. But the case was serious. Rummans had obtained medical testimony that he was disabled for life and would suffer pain and physical distress indefinitely. He was then about thirty-six years old.

The medical opinion worried me. Malpractice suits were not common then, and questioning a doctor on the witness stand was nearly always a touchy matter. Doctors are esteemed people. Of course, we would have an expert of our own. It could come down, as cases often do, to which witness impressed the jury more.

Nor did I relish going to California to try this suit, and I told McNeese so. I believed that the promoter had so wrongfully conducted himself as to deserve what McCarthy had done. But I also knew that trying a case of this kind in a foreign jurisdiction posed serious problems. We all prefer to have the home field.

The attorney representing the plaintiff was a well-known personal injury lawyer out of San Francisco. He knew all the tricks of building up a case of this kind. Judge James M. Carter, later promoted to the Circuit Court of Appeals, was to preside in district court.

As we expected, the plaintiff told a story entirely different from the version McCarthy gave. He had medical practitioners, as well as osteopaths, who testified to his disabilities.

We had our own experts who testified to the contrary. I cross-examined at length a doctor who was most fervent in his claim that the plaintiff was impaired for life.

After one of my questions, he said he would answer provided I paid him proper compensation. I countered by suggesting it would take him less than a minute to answer and how much did he expect for this period of testimony? He promptly replied that he wanted one hundred dollars. This was an error on his part. I turned and looked at the jurors. I could see the disgust on their faces. People do not take kindly to witnesses whose testimony is offered for money.

As the trial wore on, I had grown troubled by a tactic employed by the plaintiff's counsel. He would ask the witnesses, his and ours, questions that were clearly intended not to elicit information but to have a psychological effect on the jury. "And then," he coaxed one witness, "didn't McCarthy say, 'This is not the way we do things in Texas'?" Once he referred to Glenn as "Mr. Texas himself," and again as "the Sultan of Houston."

Of course, this language had nothing to do with the issues of the case. The idea was to raise the Texas stereotype: McCarthy as the arrogant Texan disregarding the rights of others.

When the last witness stepped down, the judge agreed to allow an hour and fifteen minutes to each side for oral argument. Opposing counsel devoted virtually his entire summation to an attack on the overbearing nature of Texans, their belief that they were richer and more powerful and more endowed with God's blessing than those of

less favored states, including California. He was painting a
comic strip. At any moment I expected him to break out
the old bromide "You can always tell a Texan, but you
can't tell him much."

But he was effective. I listened with some awe at the
manner in which the plaintiff's lawyer injected his bias.
Such an argument has only one design: to appeal to the
passion and prejudice of the jury. I had not expected it.

When he finished I realized that few of the points I had
prepared were now appropriate. I had to shift completely
to a different type of argument and answer him on the
basis of his attack on Texans. By now it was four-thirty in
the afternoon. My immediate fear was that the court would
adjourn and the jury would live with those poisonous
thoughts overnight. I approached the bench and asked
Judge Carter for thirty minutes in which to make my argument. I would waive the rest of my time.

The judge said he did not feel justified in keeping the
jury any later. I replied that it would be unfair to let the
jury retire for the night without an answer to this prejudicial appeal. Finally the judge said, "All right, I'll leave it
up to the jury." He turned and said, "Counsel from Texas
says he will waive the rest of his time, if you would be
willing to listen to him for thirty minutes. Is that agreeable?"

One by one the jurors nodded their assent. The judge
told me to proceed. My mind raced. No attorney likes to
stand in front of a jury, unprepared, without a note or a
plan, the outline of his case suddenly useless. One feels
naked. All I could think of was finding the words, the

thoughts, that would offset the venom that had been spread.

There is a point in every trial where the case has gone beyond tricks and fancy rhetoric. You can't hold the attention of the jury by pulling out your pocket comb and playing "The Star-Spangled Banner" on it. So I spoke softly and clearly, pacing each sentence the way a runner puts one foot in front of the other.

I wanted to appeal to their higher instincts. I began by remarking on the special nature of a system that permits strangers from Texas to travel to California, confident that fairness and justice would be observed. I noted the fairness and impartiality the judge had shown in the conduct of the trial, and the attentiveness of the jury in following the testimony. This line was more than simple flattery. I wanted to remind them that we, fifteen hundred miles from our home state, had to depend upon the uprightness of our neighbors.

Sonic travel and the advances in live television reporting have so shrunk the country that today, as never before, we feel a sense of community. But in 1951 more people still traveled by railroads than by air, and there were still cities in America without television. As I had listened to the closing argument of the plaintiff's counsel, I had thought, "That fellow is going to make me prove that Texas is a part of the United States." Now I set out to do so.

"During the war," I said, "I saw Californians and Texans train together. They marched into battle side by side. They fought side by side. They died and were buried side by side in eternal resting grounds."

I had never tried a case before to a jury of male and female jurors. All-male juries were still the custom in Texas
and a number of other states. Three women were on this
panel, and when I got to the point of the Texans and Californians dying together on the battlefield, two of them
began to cry. One was sobbing loudly enough to cause me
concern. I thought perhaps she had lost a loved one in the
war.

As I made my argument, plaintiff's counsel was on his
feet objecting repeatedly, until Judge Carter instructed
him not to interrupt me again. If he had any objections,
the judge said, he could make them when I finished.

I moved on to another point, one that I believe is at the
heart of today's wave of malpractice suits. I appealed to the
jury not to let one who had in effect faked his claims to receive a reward that would compound the wrong. I argued
that the jury could best serve the future well-being of this
man by not letting him believe that through a phony lawsuit he could gain funds to which he was not entitled.

After thirty minutes, exactly, I sat down. The judge discharged the jury and listened to the motions of my adversary, who asked the court to declare a mistrial and hold me
in contempt for my "improper" arguments. Judge Carter
overruled him.

The jury deliberated the next day for a longer period
than I had anticipated. My nervousness mounted as we
waited. I had the feeling that the best we would get was a
hung jury.

It turned out that one juror was in favor of awarding the
plaintiff some damages. All the rest were opposed. A com-

promise was reached, in which the plaintiff was given a small sum of money due under his contract with McCarthy. All of his claims for personal injury and false imprisonment were denied.

Not a demonstrative person, except in a fight, Glenn was filled with praise and appreciation. The case was the last I tried for him, and I felt the warm bond that grows between people who share interesting years. Glenn McCarthy may have been the last of that breed the wildcatter, the independent oilman who took his own risks, rolled his own dice, and didn't believe in partners.

· Today the old-school wildcatter is still the best hope of uncovering new domestic oil supplies. But the rules and the people have changed. They need government help to survive, particularly for expensive offshore and overseas operations.

As the times and the shifting search for energy drove out the lone operator, and brought on the international consortiums, Glenn McCarthy's era faded away. The courtrooms may be a little less crowded, but the oil industry is not nearly so colorful.

After the trial in California, Judge Carter said he was impressed with my closing speech to the jury. "In all my long experience," he said, "it was the first time I have seen a jury cry for a millionaire."

4

The Soldiers

I very nearly missed World War II. I do not believe the Allied victory would have been delayed in any case, but surely my career, my life, my ideas about law and justice were affected by what I saw and learned in those years.

Military justice, because it so often deals with duty and discipline, challenges the fairness of the law in ways that are less predictable than in our civilian courts. The war crimes trials were to break new ground. They established as a principle of law that every individual must take responsibility for his or her actions, even while carrying out the orders of a higher authority, if one had the ability to make a judgment that such an order was unlawful.

I had no military experience, no knowledge of that code of justice, when the bombs fell at Pearl Harbor on December 7, 1941. I was thirty-six, with three children in grade school.

As I watched friends and younger associates don their

uniforms and go off to war, I grew more and more restive. In my own mind, the only question was when I would enlist. War as a planetary adventure did not excite me. But I believed seriously in the debt I owed this country, which had embraced my parents as immigrants from Europe. I lost my mother at the age of three and grew up worshiping a father who spoke often and lyrically of his love for America. He was a learned man who spoke several languages, preached his sermons in German, and played a variety of musical instruments.

He cared alone for my two brothers and sister and me for five years, until he married a woman who lived on the farm nearest ours. Her name was Adele. She was the daughter of a Confederate soldier, and the only mother I ever knew. I loved her dearly.

The Jaworski home was built on a prairie, next to the church and across the road from the town cemetery, a beautifully groomed cemetery with lots of greenery and statuary. I would be reminded of it by many of the cemeteries I later saw in Germany.

My father would hitch up the horse and buggy and ride to neighboring towns for weddings and funerals. I would begin to worry about him if he had not returned by nightfall. But I could hear him approach even before he came into view. As the buggy would reach the crest of a hill a mile from our home, I could pick up the clippety-clop of the horse's steps along the dirt road. It was one of the great sounds of my youth. I can hear it even now in my mind.

My father came to this country because he felt the freedoms he cherished were being threatened in his native

Poland, and in all of Europe. It may sound quaint to some, but I thought I had an obligation to him, and to my childhood, to serve in the armed forces.

My wife accepted my decision quietly. She was the one who would have to manage the children, and our home, on my army pay and whatever savings we had. Jeannette never uttered a negative thought. It was not until months after the war that she told me she had suffered awful doubts, and had spent sleepless nights, worrying about my leaving my family and law practice to join a young man's war. "Now that it's over," she said, smiling, "I want to tell you that I think you made the right decision."

I felt keenly the problem of leaving my firm with a heavy docket of untried cases. I volunteered for the Army in June of 1942, two months after asking the courts in Harris County to set as many cases of mine as could be handled. From that point on, I was in court day after day, week after week, and was able virtually to clear the load I had undertaken.

I did not exactly feel light of heart about rearranging my life. The news from the Pacific was grim. Bataan and then Corregidor had fallen. The war was everything. One wanted to be in it, speeding along with it. I did not see the military experience influencing my career either way. But it never dawned on me that I would not do well, would not re-establish myself quickly, after I returned.

Routinely, I reported to Ellington Air Force Base outside of Houston for my physical, and was told I had passed. I would be commissioned as a captain.

Resigning my job, I said good-by to most of my friends

and purchased a uniform. The custom then was for the government to provide an allowance for clothing. Most of the large department stores in Houston carried officer's uniforms, and I bought mine at Battelstein's.

Then, unexpectedly, word came from Washington that my commission would be delayed. A closer look had been taken at my medical report. I was notified that my blood pressure and heartbeat were on the borderline of the limits prescribed by the Army. In view of my age, additional tests were ordered over a three-day period. I was dismayed and had visions of being rejected. What would I tell my friends? What would I do with my uniform?

My family doctor disagreed with the Army's findings. It was obvious to him, he said, that my condition was the product of trying so many cases in a crash period. He gave me a small container of pills to take before the examinations that would, as he put it, "slow me down."

A half hour before my first exam I swallowed one of the pills. Just as the medical corpsman snapped the cuff around my arm, an air raid alert sounded and all of us had to evacuate the building, run a distance, then flatten ourselves on the ground. When we returned, despite the medication my blood pressure was high, and the technician was concerned. He suggested I rest a few minutes, whereupon I asked for directions to the men's room. There I quickly washed down another of the pills.

I took my place again in the examining room. After a few minutes, I nearly went to sleep. When the technician took my blood pressure again, he did a double take. He could not believe what he read on his instruments. He called for another gauge, thinking that his had malfunctioned. This one revealed the same condition: I was darned near a victim of low blood pressure!

In any event, the exam was repeated in the afternoon and again the next morning, with acceptable results. Not wishing to press my luck, I asked the flight surgeon to excuse me from the next day and a half of tests. He looked at my chart and then, arbitrarily, filled in the spaces for the remaining tests. I was in. The records went to Washington and I received my commission as a captain in the Judge Advocate General's Corps, the legal branch of the Army.

It had not occurred to me that I had outfoxed the Army, or that the medical officer had taken liberties on my behalf. Hundreds of men were being processed daily. As they say, if you could sing and take a shower at the same time, Uncle Sam needed you. In my case, I knew I was healthy. The numbers had been deceptive; not me.

I was assigned to a special school in Washington for three months of classes in military justice, with some instruction in tactics. I was so totally ignorant of the jargon and procedures, I had never even heard of a morning report. When I finished the course, the deputy judge advocate wanted to keep me in the Pentagon at a desk job, a prospect I found disheartening. I asked to be sent into the field, where at least I could work with the troops.

Transferred to Fort Sam Houston, in San Antonio, Texas, I reported to Lieutenant Colonel Julien C. Hyer—a stranger to me then, one of my closest friends when I left the service three and a half years later. My first assignment was to work with the FBI and other civil enforcement

officers to co-ordinate the arrest, confinement, and trial of
military personnel charged with civil crimes. It was then
considered disgraceful for a man wearing a uniform to be
sitting in jail, and charged by civilian authorities, instead of
being placed in a military compound and tried by court-
martial. Throughout history, it has been an article of faith
that armies judge, and punish, their own. Legal talent is
therefore much in demand, and legal tempers often short,
because the military has a way of placing itself on trial. In
cases ranging from desertion to mass murder, from Private
Slovik to Lieutenant Calley, the system as well as the individual has stood accused

I preferred to be doing trial work, but kept my complaints to myself. Army life was still strange to me. I would
not have attempted to pull any strings, even if I had
known how. Then, quite by accident, Colonel Hyer ran
into a friend of mine, a Houston lawyer named Charles
Francis. Later, Hyer called me into his office and demanded to know why I had not told him I was an experienced trial lawyer. I said no one had ever asked.

From that time on, I tried scores of cases for the Eighth
Service Command, involving the full range of human
frailty: murder, desertion, rape, robbery, embezzlement,
forgery. No matter how serious the charge, there is often
sympathy for anyone who has been called to serve his country. I find such sympathy misplaced. I felt regret, but
mostly anger at the creative ways these men dishonored
their uniform. Soldiers, like law officers and politicians, are
figures of authority whose actions are essential to the pub-

lic order. They *must* be held accountable, swiftly and fully, for their misdeeds.

Soon I was reassigned to a number of sensitive trials. I traveled across the country to other commands, at their request, to serve as trial judge advocate. In the Army, at that time, this position compared to that of a prosecutor, except that the trial judge advocate was sworn to divulge all the facts in his possession, no matter which side was helped. The defense, meanwhile, was not permitted to resort to some stratagems used in civil trials. There was, then, almost no red tape in a court-martial. One officer, designated as the law member, advised the court on legal questions, since members of the board were not usually trained at law.

My assignment to these cases was not unusual. The practice was to bring in a trial lawyer from another post, someone not exposed to local pressures. The number of cases always exceeded the supply of lawyers to try them. Those of us whose work had become known in Washington were kept busy.

In December of 1943 I was assigned to a series of top-secret trials of German POWs for the political murders of fellow prisoners, who had been less than passionate perhaps in their loyalty to the Nazi ideals. Not many Americans were then aware that German prisoners were being held on our soil. Secrecy was necessary partly for reasons of security. We wanted no ugly incidents involving the civilian population.

Why were the trials kept secret? Why were they held in

the first place? Crimes committed by one prisoner against another are easy enough to ignore.

But there was never a question of not holding the trials. To allow those who committed violent acts to go unpunished would have been equivalent to licensing the Nazi subgovernments that operated in every camp. We had an obligation to uphold the rights of those prisoners then under our protection.

The Army was not anxious to publicize the whereabouts of the German POWs. We did not want to appear to be using the trials for propaganda reasons, or to turn them into public spectacles. Intramural murder is an especially nasty business, and anti-Nazi emotions were feverish enough.

In keeping the trials secret, the government was taking a calculated risk. We had to be certain that they did not seem to be inquisitions. A representative of the Swiss government was to be present throughout. He would deliver a record of the proceedings to the German authorities. It was crucial that no doubts exist about the fairness of the trials. We knew how eagerly the Nazis could misuse the record for their own propaganda.

More important, some of our fliers were in the enemy's hands, and the risk of reprisal against them troubled us. This made us all the more determined to let the trial record speak clearly and convincingly.

In one of these cases, at Camp Chaffee, Arkansas, a German soldier named Heller, only twenty-one, was beaten to death after volunteering for work not required by the Geneva Convention, but for which he was paid. Someone in the camp decided that an example had to be made of young Heller, as a warning to others not to co-operate with their captors.

The next evening, as Heller was in his barracks tinkering with a radio, another prisoner appeared at the door. He asked if anyone in the room had lived in Sundheim, Germany. He added that there was a comrade at the fence between the two compounds who wished to speak with anyone from this town. Heller spoke up, said Sundheim was his home, and then followed the man out into the darkness. As they neared the fence, six assailants emerged from behind one of the buildings and pounced on Heller, beating him with clubs and other blunt instruments. He died that night.

I was assigned to investigate the killing, identify the ringleaders, and bring them to trial.

Hours of interviews with the men in the barracks shed very little light. I pored over the camp records. I began with two basic questions: Who knew Heller's personal history? Who would have known that he had volunteered to work for the Americans?

I studied the photograph of Heller. He was nice-looking, dark-haired, with a thin, sensitive face, remindful of the actor Montgomery Clift. He had sought the extra work to send money home to his bride. Surely there were some among the prisoners who did not condone this vicious act.

Those prisoners who seemed weak or nervous, or were suspected of having information, I immediately had isolated from their comrades. Such a procedure was routine.

If they had any kind of conscience, solitary confinement gave it a chance to work.

I made it a practice to question them through an interpreter, even though I spoke German and understood what they were saying. The presence of a third party was to discourage claims of mistreatment. I never abused a suspect or raised a hand to one, although at times their arrogance made me want to slap them silly.

German prisoners had made monkeys out of many an American investigator. Before I arrived at Camp Chaffee, one had professed to know the killer and offered to point him out in a line-up. A "dental inspection" was arranged. A large room was divided by a screen, equipped with a peephole, through which the informant would watch as the other prisoners, three or four hundred of them, would file toward the dental chair. They would be grinning and laughing. Hours later, the informant would turn to our people, shrug, and say he didn't see the assassin.

After several days of questioning, I began to get a few answers. Two or three prisoners obviously had more information than they were revealing, and I had them transferred to other camps, where they could talk more freely. Slowly, my suspicions focused on two others as having masterminded the killing. Their names were Herbert Messer and Emil Ludwig.

Messer was a fine specimen, six foot one, blond and blue-eyed. He was a sergeant and, like most of the NCOs captured in North Africa, represented the cream of the German Army. Messer maintained the records of each prisoner, meaning that he knew the town from which Heller came. Ludwig had a job in the infirmary and would have been in a position to observe Heller at work. As I was to learn later, Ludwig informed Messer, who carefully picked and organized a detail whose special assignment was to beat Heller into submission. He had a term of reference for those he sought to punish: the Heilige Geist (Holy Ghost) would wait on them.

I questioned Messer at length on several occasions. He was a sharp and cunning young man of twenty-six, a super-patriot who followed the Nazi line more seriously than most. I made little headway in obtaining any incriminating admissions from him, but I became convinced that he was the key figure. The other prisoners seemed to fear him. He had a taunting, cat-and-mouse attitude, daring us to prove him guilty. "No one will talk," he told me at one point. "You have nothing. You can prove nothing."

Somehow I needed to break through his shell of smugness. During one interview, in an effort to test his re-actions, I spoke with disdain of the Nazi ideology. This man who had amazed me with his composure now lost his calm and even manner. Nothing I could say about him per-sonally could cause so much as an eyelid to flutter. But to hear anyone speak ill of the Nazi cause was unbearable to him. He squirmed. His mouth contorted. He blustered.

Messer had been a leader of the Hitler Jugend (Hitler Youth) in his section of Germany. He attempted to per-suade me, at one point, that the Hitler Jugend was no different from the Boy Scouts of America. That compari-son would have been funny, had it been less contrived. The record was already clear: these German lads, from their early teens, had been taught to be tough and pitiless, to hate and to terrify.

The murder of Heller had been arranged at a time when Messer was holding an indoctrination with some of his fellow prisoners. Thus he had an alibi and a number of witnesses to establish it. Yet I was convinced that he was the mastermind, and had assembled persuasive, if circumstantial, proof of his guilt. The fact that he did not participate in the actual violence on Heller would not save him from prosecution, if it could be shown that he was a party to the conspiracy.

All during this time I harbored a strong hunch that Ludwig had assisted Messer by serving as his "lookout" in the infirmary. However, I had little or no proof against him and, on the surface, he seemed an unlikely suspect. He had been an ordained minister before entering the German Army. He was a model prisoner of war, quiet, polite, obedient, and faultless in his demeanor. Still, the hunch was strong.

Finally, in an effort to exhaust all the possibilities, I ordered Ludwig placed in isolation, then had his quarters searched. I was fishing, looking for evidence, hoping perhaps to find one of the weapons used to kill Heller. The Germans would take a two-by-four, sandpaper and whittle a handle, and use it as a club.

We didn't find the club, but we did discover a fascinating document. It was a diary Ludwig had kept of his experiences at the camp, in the form of a daily letter addressed to his wife in Germany. He had concealed it well, but the MPs who searched his room found it.

I read the diary with searching interest. It contained remarkable disclosures. On those occasions when a prisoner of war was beaten by others for failing to observe the Nazi code, Ludwig recorded the details with gloating satisfaction. He described the suffering and agony of the victims, and expressed his pleasure that such an efficient job was being done of punishing any "defectors." The more blood and gore, the better he seemed to like it.

I questioned other prisoners who had served with him about Ludwig's past. Yes, he had been at one time a highly respected minister of the gospel. I read and reread his diary: how he was captured, his impressions of this country, how he felt about the attacks on the other POWs. I came to know him.

He was taken prisoner less than a month after landing in North Africa. His unit was pinned down and cut to pieces by a British mortar attack. They retreated, then tried to follow a dry river bed, hoping to find a squad of paratroopers. Instead, Ludwig and a friend wandered into a British patrol. He was turned over to the French and then to the Americans.

> March 26, 1943
> Another interrogation. I already can tell by the captain's nose what kind of race he belongs to. He is questioning me about religion and philosophy. But I was not intimidated by his questions and [that] made him more and more furious. I was amused by this whole game. . . . We reached our next destination, Souk-Ahras. Heavily guarded, we were marched through the town. The town was full of Jews and we received some hateful glances. We were

called "German pigs" and similar names. But we proudly marched on, although dirty and unshaven. . . .

On April 8, with 1,600 Italian prisoners and 196 of his fellow Germans, Ludwig sailed on an American flagship for New York. From there they traveled by train to their final destination, Camp Chaffee. The thoughts Ludwig revealed to his wife were more those of a tourist than a prisoner of war.

April 29, 1943

Of course, we were curious what the land of unlimited possibilities would look like. However, we were very disappointed about the things we saw. The train traveled for some time through the suburbs of New York. On one side were the skyscrapers and on the other side the worst slums: wooden houses, dark, narrow, and dirty streets. This is America? Poor America. Places like this I had not seen in Germany. All around us we only saw wooden houses, mostly huts, but a fantastic car was always parked in front of them. And this scenery did not change; throughout Virginia, Tennessee, and Arkansas we saw huge, poorly cultivated fields, and forests, ugly towns with wooden houses, but always cars!

May 1, 1943

We finally reach our destination, Camp Chaffee. A huge compound. Close to it is our camp. Thirty guards are responsible for fifty prisoners. Are we really that dangerous or are they only afraid of us? The camp consists of three large, separate compounds. Each compound can house up to 1,000 men. We are assigned to Compound B. Three companies are already there and we are greeted with the Nazi greeting. . . . Resembling a triumphant march we are led to our quarters.

The summer months passed quietly for Ludwig. The
food was so plentiful and nourishing, he wrote his wife
that he wished he could send some of it home to her. He
had gained weight. And he and his comrades had not lost
their confidence or their convictions.

October 27, 1943

Everything has settled into a routine. We have a self-
government. Sometimes it becomes difficult to work with
the Americans because of daily disagreements. Especially
when they ask for something which is not compatible with
the German military honor. . . . In any case, we are not
intimidated by the Americans; they are afraid of us! Impossible things have happened. Daily some men were
needed to work in the quarry or in the lumberyard. One
day the men went on strike because they felt threatened
by the loaded guns of the guards. What were the guards
supposed to do? They emptied their rifles and shotguns
but this still did not satisfy the men. Not until the German officer convinced himself that the rifles and guns were
empty did the men continue their work. Can you imagine
that? The men started to strike for any reason. We were
not afraid of anything. They wanted to prohibit us from
using the Hitler salute. We succeeded in getting permission to salute in our usual manner. Each [American] officer
is saluted with raised hand; to his anger and our delight.
At the appropriate occasions we sang our national hymns.
Each prisoner has the Swastika on his uniform. We still
remain German soldiers even in captivity. Those who do
not subject themselves to our old principles and order *are*
rejected from our community. This happened to the trai-
tors, deserters, and communists.

November 2, 1943

Among us were some former Poles and Austrians who
had deserted! They were supposed to be taken care of

[killed], but the Americans rescued them in time. But first we really beat them up until they were bleeding when the Americans got them.

The Americans are very afraid of the *Rabatz* [small riot]. When things do not go our way we make a *Rabatz*. For example, the "Black Hand" would come at night. . . . During these incidents the Yankees were forced to post guards around the entire camp. They stood five to six yards apart from each other pointing their weapons at us. We only laughed at them. The Americans hope to destroy our Nazi convictions with these measures. How these poor devils deceived themselves. They really do not know us at all. They are still under the impression that they are dealing with a Germany of 1918.

Of course, there were no entries dealing with the death of Heller. Ludwig had not revealed much, but it was enough. He had gloated over the riots and the discipline of the Black Hand. I knew how his mind worked, which is the most important edge an investigator can have.

Finally, I was ready to talk with Ludwig. Hidden in my briefcase was his diary. We spoke of many things. I asked him about his youth, his education, his preparation for the ministry, the sacrifices such a calling entailed. I explained that I shared some knowledge of the subject because my father was a retired Protestant minister.

Then we came to the subject of the assaults and the killings that had taken place among his comrades.

"How sad and deplorable it was," I commented. He agreed.

"Something must be done about it," I added. Again, he readily agreed.

"It must be particularly odious to you—a man of the cloth."

Ludwig nodded, playing the role of one deeply saddened over incidents so terrible, yet beyond his control. He spoke of his helplessness. "After all," he observed, "it is too late to change my comrades."

Some of my interviews with Messer had lasted hours, had turned intense and brought both of us to a physical and mental sweat. But now, as this act of Ludwig's went on for a length of time, I experienced the sensation of an actor about to make his best move to an audience totally unprepared.

I reached into my briefcase, slowly removed his diary and placed it on the table in front of him. For a period that probably lasted two minutes, but may have seemed like hours to Ludwig, I fixed my eyes on him. He soon became uncomfortable. I asked him for an explanation. The most he could say was, "You just do not understand."

That was true. I did not understand. It was beyond my power of comprehension to think of this man, once a minister, now encouraging violence and death. I could better understand after I landed in Germany and dealt with others of his kind.

I was still confronted with the problem of getting witnesses to talk, and then producing them before a court-martial to testify to the roles of Messer and Ludwig. The problem seemed insurmountable.

My best hope for such a witness was one of the German soldiers I had placed in isolation, a man named Abar, the top-ranking enlisted man in the compound where the killing occurred. I had him transferred to a hospital, where I could ensure his safety. There I would see him for thirty minutes or an hour in the morning, and sometimes again in the afternoon. He seemed to enjoy these visits. Captured soldiers often make a game out of matching wits with their interrogators. I usually brought him candy and gum and cigarettes. Once he gave me a snapshot he had taken of Field Marshal Rommel, under whom he had served in North Africa.

He talked freely, except on the subject in which I was most interested. After several days, Abar said that my efforts to question him on the beatings in the compound made him quite nervous. He had been thinking the matter over, he said. As the ranking NCO he had decided he should take the blame. He had written a statement and was prepared to accept whatever punishment followed.

There was no evidence, and little in his character, to indicate that Abar had been involved. He was a professional soldier, not a Nazi fanatic. There was no arrogance in him. He always clicked his heels and snapped to attention when I walked into his room. I refused to accept his statement and told him that any effort on his part to shield others would not end the investigation.

I continued to visit Abar. Finally I decided to play a long shot. I asked him if he would agree to let me question him under the influence of a truth serum. Of course, whatever he said would be useless to me as evidence in court, but that was not my purpose. I needed to confirm my strong suspicions of Messer.

Abar was advised, both by me and by an army doctor, of the usual effects of truth serum: that his inhibitions about discussing the violence would likely be removed. He agreed to its use. Why, I am unable to say for certain. Perhaps he wanted to co-operate and saw this technique as a way to cover himself. Or perhaps he simply welcomed another, interesting turn in the clash of wits.

After receiving the approval of the commanding general of the Eighth Service Command, I arranged with an officer in the Medical Corps—one experienced in such matters—to administer the injection. The doctor made it clear to me that I had to talk to Abar constantly and somewhat loudly, otherwise he would fall asleep.

Truth serum was a potion usually associated with "spooks," the spy services. I considered its use in this case an experiment and went to my task with heightened senses. For thirty minutes, with Abar somewhat unsteady in his chair, I questioned him with more success than I had anticipated. He was not an eyewitness to the killing of Heller, but Messer had told him of the vicious work his goon squad had done. Whatever doubt there might have been in my mind about Messer's guilt was removed. Suddenly, Abar announced that he was sleepy and wanted to go to bed. I told him to go right ahead, and immediately he fell over and went into a sound sleep.

The next morning, a Sunday, when I entered Abar's room he arose, walked to the window, and silently turned his back on me. He had revealed himself to me and now, on second thought, he wished he had not done so. He hated himself for disclosing these facts, and he hated me for having suggested that he submit to the serum. He would not speak to me that morning.

I returned in the afternoon, and when I offered him the candy and cigarettes I had brought he refused them. Unless I regained his confidence, I knew all of my effort would be to no avail. I decided to wait until Monday to approach him.

When I appeared that morning, I pulled up a chair close to him and asked that he listen carefully to what I had to say. I reminded him of the confession he had tendered to me; how I could have turned it over to my superiors, and received much credit, with the result that he would have been on trial accused of murder. I added that in my opinion he would have received the death penalty. I then asked whether he thought I had dealt fairly with him or unfairly, whether I was someone he could afford to trust. I pointed out that by questioning him under the influence of the serum I was able to clear him fully, and at the same time begin to fix the responsibility where it belonged. Then I left.

I did not return in the afternoon. The next morning I found him friendlier. Within a few days he was ready to co-operate. He agreed to testify in court. I promised him not only that I would find ways of guarding him properly, but that he would eventually be moved to other camps far away, and no prisoners from Chaffee would ever be transferred to a camp where he was sent.

Abar had no way of knowing exactly what he had told

me. But after I regained his confidence he revealed all he
knew, and at my request reduced his information to writing. What he told me matched without deviation what he
had revealed while in a subconscious state. And when Abar
appeared as a witness in court he repeated these facts. His
testimony withstood a withering cross-examination by the
defense counsel.

During the trial, Messer, in a clear attempt to intimidate
Abar, took copious notes on Abar's testimony: his way of
letting the witness know he would have to answer for his
disloyalty. The implication was that Messer would find a
way of getting these notes into the hands of others, who
would someday have their revenge.

Messer received the death sentence by general court-martial. On review, because the case was circumstantial his sentence was reduced to a long term of confinement at Fort
Leavenworth. I kept my promise to Abar. The notes were
destroyed, and he was given protection and transferred to a
small camp far from Camp Chaffee.

Much to my regret, I could not obtain legal proof
sufficient to convict Ludwig, so no charges were filed
against him. But his diary justified his transfer to another
POW camp where, instead of a position of trust, he received the bare minimum of rights and benefits due him
under the Geneva Convention.

The investigation and trial consumed months of effort to
bring to justice German prisoners, for the killing of one of
their own. Was the time and effort worthwhile? Absolutely. We can never afford to devalue human life. Law

agencies launch massive sweeps to solve gangland slayings, knowing that we cannot allow ourselves to say, even to the sub-layers of society: "What you do is all right, as long as you do it to each other."

5

War Crimes

⚛

At Christmas 1944 I was told to stand by for orders overseas.

After reporting to the office of the judge advocate general, in Washington, I began to mark time. Days passed. Rumors reached me through friends that I would be appointed to head the war crimes section for the European theater. I sat at a desk, waiting, hearing nothing.

Although the idea of taking part in the war crimes trials appealed to me, I did not lobby for it. I had seen the futility of that course all around me. There was some truth to the joke that soldiers who asked for combat duty ended up as cooks, and vice versa.

Then I received a letter from a friend in Paris, an officer on Eisenhower's staff, telling me what the hitch was. Washington could send no one to that theater, in the technical services, without a request by General Eisenhower.

And Ike's judge advocate, General Betts, a West Point man, wanted one of his own.

I could appreciate his problem. West Point is the Mother Temple of the American military. It is, or was, one of the great and exclusive clubs, and its members stick together. I do not intend that reference in an unflattering way. But sooner or later, every civilian-soldier runs up against the West Point ceiling.

Career men know that, in wartime, where you serve is nearly as important as how. I was just another temporary soldier who would be going home, and returning to civil law. But there were historic cases coming in Europe. I didn't plan to make the Army my life, but I wanted in on them. You may not believe in beauty contests, but if you enter one you want to be voted pretty.

When no request came from Eisenhower's office, a plan was concocted, unknown to me, in the office of the deputy judge advocate general. All of the top-secret records on war crimes had to be shipped to Paris, some 132 pounds of them. It was decided that I would personally accompany the records and deliver them to General Betts, impressing him, it was hoped, with the confidence Washington had in me.

The war was in its final stages. I went by plane from Washington to Newfoundland to the Azores and then to Orly Airfield. It was nearly midnight when I landed in Paris, and I still had to deposit my trunk of records in a vault before I could check into my hotel room. I finally staggered into my room well after one o'clock in the morning. I kicked off my shoes, sat on the edge of the bed, stared at the floor, and wondered what I was doing there. After a few hours of sleep, I took the métro to report to General Betts. He received me coldly, plainly annoyed by what he regarded as pressure from Washington. My response was brief. "General Betts," I said, "I'm here to help in this effort. I do not care how menial the assignment may be. Can't we brush all that aside and you just put me where you want."

I was a lieutenant colonel then. The general assigned me to an office shared by four full colonels. The message was not subtle.

Before long, however, I was placed in charge of the division responsible for examining the evidence relating to war crimes. Our procedures were still being determined. It was all new ground. For one thing, there was still no agreement among the Allies on what to do with war criminals or how to do it. The Russians were reported to have hanged a few as they went along, but no one could be certain. But every day we were adding more names and deeds to our catalogue of Nazi war crimes. Some of our information came from prisoners who had escaped and some from repatriates.

After a few weeks, I was given an additional duty: to head the division investigating the cases. General Betts had accepted me. Funny thing about the Army. Sometimes a man moves up more quickly when it becomes obvious that he is not ambitious. I was there to work, not win a promotion, and I would hope that I got that idea across. Two of the colonels whose space I shared were soon moved into the field. I formed a friendship with another colonel, Clio

E. Straight, who was able and sensitive and knowledgeable in army ways. He guided me and, above all, believed in me.

Those months in Paris were spent digging through notebooks and files and documents, case histories that turned your stomach or made you want to weep. I had no social life of any kind. As the war moved away from us, and the pockets of resistance dwindled, many officers had little to do in the evenings but sit around and drink, and enjoy what company they could find. I listened with amusement to the exaggerated stories, and some not so exaggerated, as my friends told how they had earned their hangovers. In my case my nights were not long enough—spent reading about strangers I could hardly wait to meet.

Early on the morning of May 1, in a late snowfall that left Paris wearing a beautiful mantle of white, I had boarded a plane for London. I had been summoned to review the films taken by the Allied forces as they entered the concentration camps in Germany. Enough footage had been taken to occupy an audience for six days. At the end of the first day, I was not certain I could continue, so dispirited, even distraught, had those pictures left me.

I saw the celebration of V-E Day in London on the afternoon of May 8, and again in the evening in Paris. That night, with Clio Straight, I strolled along the Champs Élysées and witnessed a celebration probably unparalleled in history.

When our staff moved into Germany, and established headquarters at Wiesbaden, we began thinking in terms of the trials. The questions consumed us: Who would prosecute these cases? Who would head the war crimes trial section? Soon enough we knew. I was appointed as executive officer, which placed me second in command, under a colonel, a regular army man, with no courtroom experience. A few months later I was promoted to chief of the section.

Although *all* war crimes trials in the European theater are commonly referred to today as the Nuremberg Trials, the cases against Hermann Göring and the other Nazi Reich masters did not come to court until November 20, 1945.

Four months earlier, in the American zone, our staff prosecuted the first war crimes trials since the adoption of the Geneva Convention in 1929. I had received orders in July to bring to justice the persons responsible for the death march of eight American fliers. They had been stoned to death on the streets of Rüsselsheim by a civilian mob, whose leaders included two women.

After we moved into Germany, we were acquiring daily the names of witnesses who could testify to the atrocities we had been documenting for months. In the Rüsselsheim case, a mystery of sorts presented itself when the bodies of the American airmen were disinterred at the Rüsselsheim cemetery. An army pathologist examined the wounds and a reburial was arranged at the American Army's cemetery at Bensheim.

But we had discovered only six bodies. Our information made clear that there had been eight victims.

This was the story pieced together by our investigative team, directed by Major Luke Rogers, of New York: In August of 1944, eight members of our Air Force, on a mis-

sion over northern Germany, were shot down and captured
near Hannover. They were to be transported by train to a
camp near Frankfurt, guarded by two German soldiers. On
the outskirts of Rüsselsheim, site of the Opel Works, it became necessary to march them through town to board another train. Some of the tracks had been bombed out of
commission.

They never made it. As they marched through the
streets, a crowd gathered and began to pelt them with
stones. The captured airmen tried to shield each other.
They stumbled and fell. Cries of "Beat them to death; beat
them to pieces" were heard. The voices of the women were
unmistakable. Like animals, the crowd closed in. After two
hours of continuous beatings, the prisoners were bloody
and still. A man later identified as Joseph Hartgen, the
town propaganda leader, pulled out a pistol and pumped
several bullets into the tangled, lifeless bodies. Someone
produced a pushcart from a nearby farm and the Americans were wheeled to the cemetery, to be buried in a common grave the next day.

We interviewed several eyewitnesses, then rounded up
ten suspects, including the two women, sisters. In the general confusion of Germany's collapse, Hartgen had eluded
us. We began to comb the country for him. Incredibly,
within days, I received word that he had been found. My
excitement was mixed with disbelief. Nothing happened .
that fast—not in Europe, in 1945. But they—the intelligence people—had found our man. Hartgen was flown to
Wiesbaden and, on my orders, brought directly to an inter-
rogation room on the first floor of the jail.

I questioned him in German. Hartgen was forty-one, of average size although solidly built, with blond hair and steel-blue eyes. He was a hard-bitten Nazi. One by one I handed him the statements of those who had witnessed his brutal act. After the first few he scoffed, blamed the charges on his political enemies, suggested I was stupid to rely on such flimsy evidence. As I continued to hand him more statements, he fell into complete silence.

I had Hartgen and his belongings carefully searched. The Führer and Himmler and Goebbels had taken their lives, and some of the Nazi underlings had attempted to emulate their heroes. It was about noon when I left Hartgen. He was grim and shaken. I gave him several sheets of paper and a pencil and suggested that he write his own version of what had happened to the American fliers. I said I would return at three o'clock.

Two hours later, in the midst of a meeting, I had a strong urge to return immediately to Hartgen's cell. Breaking off in the middle of the session, I called my driver and hurried to the Wiesbaden jail. I sent an interpreter to bring the prisoner to me, and within a matter of seconds I heard shouts from an upper story. The interpreter had found Joseph Hartgen lying on the floor in a pool of blood. I took the stairs two at a time, rushed into his room, and found him semiconscious. Next to him was one of the sheets of paper I had given him, now splattered with blood. Across it he had written the words "Heil Deutschland! I will reveal nothing."

Prompt medical attention saved his life. Within a few days he was back in jail. How had he attempted suicide?

Everything in the room except a bed, a table, and a chair had been removed. But there were springs under the mattress. Hooking his wrists on the sharp edge of the coils of the bedsprings, he had jerked his arms back and forth and, in agony, managed to slash his wrists. He would have bled to death had he gone undiscovered.

Hartgen was placed under constant guard, and charged with murder along with the other ten accused.

Because only six bodies were recovered—even though all the witnesses testified there were eight airmen—the charges filed specified that they had participated in the murder of six American soldiers. The trial began on July 25, 1945, at Darmstadt, Germany, before a military commission headed by Brigadier General Garrison Davidson, later the commandant of West Point.

The accused were defended by a team led by an American officer of rank equal to mine, Lieutenant Colonel Roger E. Titus of Massachusetts, and a German attorney of their choice, Heinrich Von Bentrano, later the foreign minister for West Germany.

One of the defendants was found not guilty. Hartgen and six others, including the two women, were sentenced to death. One received twenty-five years at hard labor, and the other two each a term of fifteen years.

The trial was covered by leading American newspapers, magazines, and wire services. A few weeks later, General Davidson called me to say that he had just received an almost incredible message. It was from the two missing airmen. This was their story:

After the bodies of all eight had been placed on the

pushcart, one of them was still conscious. In fact, throughout this ordeal he never lost consciousness. Another, although still alive, had passed out. The other six were dead. When the pushcart reached the cemetery, an air raid alert sounded and those around the cart fled to seek safety. The alert was a long one. As nightfall came, both men, now fully conscious, though in pain, left the cart and hid in the chapel in the cemetery.

Later that night, in the pitch darkness of the wartime blackout, they escaped from Rüsselsheim and for several days continued to flee until they were picked up by a German patrol. They were then confined in a prisoner-of-war camp, where they remained until our troops liberated them in the final days of the German collapse. Released, they returned to their homes.

Partly to protect the loved ones of the murdered boys, they had vowed never to reveal to anyone the horror of their experience at Rüsselsheim. However, after the newspapers carried the names of their slain comrades, there was no purpose in maintaining their secret. They came forward. And so ended our Case of the Missing Airmen.

When the trial ended and Hartgen had been sentenced to death, I directed that his guards be removed. The verdict had been brought. He was left free to choose his course. He made no further attempt to take his life. Hartgen died on the gallows with a passage from the scriptures on his lips.

Such trials were troubling and distasteful. Given the temper of that time, it required no legal magic to convict these admitted Nazis, before an American tribunal and a war-shocked German jury. Our test was to be fair: to seek justice, not vengeance. I believe we met that test. But as each new case turned up evidence more grisly than the last, it became an exercise of greater will. And so, a few weeks later, we moved on to a town called Hadamar, which was situated a few miles from the city of Limburg. The only thing that distinguished Hadamar from other small German towns was the presence of a sanatorium for the mentally ill.

As early as 1941 euthanasia—the so-called mercy death—was administered there to incurable mental patients. This practice had the approval of the Third Reich, which felt it was economically unsound to provide food and shelter for such people. So proficient did the staff become that by 1944 the Nazi high command had turned the hospital at Hadamar into one of the most cold-blooded murder mills ever known.

After American troops entered the town in March of 1945, reports were received of the mass murders of Polish and Russian slave laborers. An investigation established that the reports were true. Although the victims were nationals of our allies, it was determined that jurisdiction in the case rested with the American forces.

In September a violation of international law was filed against seven staff members of the sanatorium, "in the killing of human beings of Polish and Russian nationality, their exact names and number being unknown but aggregating in excess of four hundred. . . ."

The victims numbered many more, but our proof was limited to some four hundred.

The crime was a heinous one. Involving as it did the principles of medicine and international law, the trial attracted considerable attention. Representatives of most of the Allied nations attended, including a Russian delegation of high-ranking officers.

Finding out exactly what had happened at Hadamar was not difficult. The accused spoke freely. They had kept detailed records. In the beginning, they were sent only the sickly among the Polish and Russian slave laborers, those who were half-starved and ill clothed and no longer able to perform hard labor. As time went on, those in charge of the transports became less selective. Men and women with minor ailments, and in some instances no ailments at all, were included.

Upon arrival at Hadamar, these doomed souls were told that they were to receive medication. Some were told they were being inoculated against disease. They were taken into wardrooms, were put to bed, and shortly thereafter received drugs in lethal doses, either by hypodermic needle or by mouth. As many as seventy would be brought by truck at one time, and all would be put to death within hours.

The building itself resembled a morgue, gloomy and forbidding. Most of the rooms were small, cold, and bleak. There was little furniture other than beds and these, without exception, were old and uncomfortable.

The administrator of the hospital was a man named Alfons Klein. The physician in charge was Adolf Wahlmann. The two male nurses who administered the lethal doses were Heinrich Ruoff and Karl Willig. The chief female nurse, who assisted the others, was Irmgard Huber. A

clerk named Adolf Merkle kept the office records. Philipp
Blum, a nephew of Klein's, helped Ruoff and Willig dispose of the bodies in mass graves.

No one denied what had occurred. Their defense was
twofold: first, that this method of disposing of the victims
had the approval of higher authority; and, next, that had
they refused to carry out their orders they would have been
punished, possibly even sentenced to a concentration
camp.

The latter defense was clearly an afterthought. In none
of the statements given or written before the trial had any
of the accused claimed their actions resulted from a fear of
punishment. As to the first defense, none of them had ever
received orders from a higher authority for these execu-
tions. A stark fact soon developed: such killings had become an accepted practice at other places. When the transports arrived at Hadamar it was *assumed* that all arrivals
were to be put to death. There were no facilities for the
treatment of the ill.

In short, murder in wholesale quantities was being committed daily at Hadamar. The accused knew what they
were doing, and continued from week to week and month
to month to participate in these murders.

Each defendant took the witness stand during the trial.
Their testimony carried a similar thread, a certain detach-
ment, a coldness, a grudging regret. There was Alfons
Klein:

Q. Did it affect your feelings or emotions or your conscience to watch these injections?

A. It is not a very nice thing for a man to see those people die.

Q. Not only is it not a very nice thing, but you felt also that it was wrong, did you not?

A. Yes.

And Adolf Wahlmann, the doctor:

Q. Did it ever occur to you that some of these Russians and Poles who were killed in your institution may have been afraid of death?

A. Yes, but my death comes closer to me.

And Ruoff, the male nurse:

Q. What would you say to these people as you came into the bedrooms and prepared to inject them with this deadly drug?

A. We told them it was for treatment of their lung disease.

Q. You also injected several little children, did you not?

A. Yes.

Q. You could not give them any explanation of what you were doing to them, could you?

A. That is impossible.

Former friends testified for Irmgard Huber, the nurse, relating instances of kindness shown by her in the past. Yet she had found it simple to be associated with mass killings, including two small children she had injected herself on Christmas Day. By the time she was brought to trial she must have realized the depth of her depravity. On cross-examination she broke down and cried uncontrollably.

Of all the experiences I had in trying war crimes, Hadamar was unquestionably the most depressing. I simply could not fathom the drastic changes that could take place in human beings over a brief period of years.

At times, women slave laborers sent to Hadamar took their children with them. The children were put to death alongside their mothers. No distinctions were drawn. All who entered the sanatorium's portals met sudden death, whether young or old, sick or hearty, Catholic or Protestant. Jews were disposed of elsewhere.

The records kept by Merkle were instrumental in gaining the convictions. When a large number of victims arrived in one group, he was given a list of names in alphabetical order. He would falsify the cause of death, usually citing pneumonia or tuberculosis, as well as the dates. He did not want his records to show the incriminating fact of so many deaths on any one day. So he would take a few names at a time and show them as having died over a period of days. He was hardly as crafty as he thought. By taking the names from the top of the list, he had his "inmates" dying in alphabetical order.

I felt, as I have not felt before or since, a cold rage as I made my closing argument to the court:

"In contrast to the fairness of this proceeding, let us pause to consider what sort of a trial these accused gave to those unfortunate people who appeared before them at Hadamar between July, 1944, and April, 1945. There came person after person, weary, heavy-laden, some very sick. But they came thinking that they saw upon the horizon the dawn of a brighter day. And what sort of a trial was given them, what sort of a hearing, what sort of an opportunity was accorded them at this place where they thought they might find some comfort? . . .

"They were brought into the death halls. They were given the promise that medication would be administered to them to help them in their ailment. Oh, what a vicious falsehood, what a terrible lie, what an evil and wicked thing to do to a person who is already suffering and already carrying burdens, to build up false hope that a ray of sunshine was to enter their hearts. Yes, they were given medications, of poison that gripped their heart and closed their eyelids still. What sort of a trial did they have? Upon them was forced the hush of death. Their bodies were taken to a bleak cellar. They were lumped together and dumped together in a common grave, buried without the benefit of clergy. Now, that, in substance, is the sort of trial that the accused gave to those who appeared before *their* Bar of Justice."

The administrator, Klein, and the two male nurses were sentenced to death. The rest received sentences ranging from twenty-five years (Irmgard Huber) to life in prison (Dr. Wahlmann).

By the time of the Hadamar trial, I had accumulated enough service time under the Army's "point system" to be discharged. But I agreed to stay on long enough to help prepare the case against those in charge of the Dachau concentration camp, whose very name is now synonymous with torture and death and human ovens.

Day after day, I had been exposed to stories of tragedy and sights of horror. I wanted it to end as soon as possible.

I was eagerly awaiting the hour when I could rejoin my family and return to the practice of civil law. But Dachau was still before me.

A film on Dachau was among those I had reviewed in London, in the early stages of our war crimes investigation. Some of those scenes I was soon to see in person. Others were described to me by some of the wasted victims of the camp.

Concentration camps had been used by a few other nations in the past. But it was left to the Nazis to turn them into an instrument as ghastly as any of their weapons. The camps were designed to dispose of all who held beliefs contrary to the Nazi ideology.

Dachau was by no means the worst, although it was painful to believe that there were others more degenerate. Ironically, it was built on the outskirts of the city of Munich, referred to so often by Germans as the center of their country's culture.

I brought together my assistants to develop a plan of investigation. Then we began with massive interviews, of those suspected of committing atrocities and those who had endured and witnessed them. The functionaries who operated the camp and their underlings were also questioned at length.

Finding evidence was not our problem. It was everywhere. The task was to collect, weigh, and organize it.

When our troops first entered Dachau, the sight so shocked and sickened them that many battle-hardened veterans had to be restrained from shooting some of the offenders on the spot. What they saw was almost beyond belief. There were mothers at the point of starvation. Girls young in age but old in appearance. Young men now physically emaciated and mentally disturbed. All were deprived of the most basic sanitation.

My own first visit to Dachau, soon after it was liberated by our troops, left me numb. I feel the effects to this day. The natural aversion I had to violence was heightened by what I saw there. I refuse to watch movies or television shows that depict murder or torture. I have seen Dachau. It was enough for my lifetime.

The evidence showed that the camp, constructed to house 8,000 inmates, held some 33,000 by April of 1945. The inmates were beaten, tortured, and starved as a matter of routine. They were subjected to agonizing experiments. In one, the victim was placed in a device that enabled the doctors to observe his or her reaction to extreme changes of air pressure. Many died of hemorrhage and embolism.

In the cold water experiment, the victims were immersed in freezing water for as long as thirty-six hours, again to test their reactions. Many died from exposure.

In the salt water experiment, inmates were fed salt water for as long as five days. The doctors conducted other experiments on various body organs and tested their resistance to certain drugs.

But surely the worst terror was not knowing from day to day when the hour of death would come. As one inmate testified:

"The most terrifying memory I have relates to the continual roll call, when we would stand outside naked in the wintertime, waiting for the doctor to come down the line and point out a physically infirm person for execution."

At the end of our investigation, forty officers, doctors, and guards were charged with the murders of the victims of Dachau. I had completed my last assignment. The prosecution of the charges was placed in the hands of the capable officers who had assisted in the investigation.

The trial began on November 15, 1945, and ended on December 13. Of the forty accused, all were convicted, and thirty-six sentenced to death by hanging. Appeals for clemency were made in several cases by a defendant's wife or mother. In almost every appeal, stress was laid on "the good husband" and "the good son" he had always been.

In a review of the trial of the men who operated Dachau, Colonel C. B. Mickelwait wrote: "The exact number of inmates will probably never be known. Neither will the numbers among them who were starved, beaten, tortured and died. The evidence in the record . . . shows beyond all doubt that no one who entered its gates as an inmate escaped some degree of mistreatment. That in their manner of operating Dachau, and in the practices which they tolerated . . . and perpetrated there, those persons responsible for its daily operation were guilty of war crimes is clear. This conclusion is obvious from several facts which are nowhere denied by any of the accused."

Justice Robert Jackson and Colonel Robert G. Storey, of the Nuremberg prosecution staff, had filed a request with the Army to make me available at Nuremberg. With only slight reluctance, I said no, and held to my agreement. I

had seen and heard enough. I was ready for my discharge
and a prompt return to the United States.

I had two other reasons for not staying. My father was in
poor health (he passed away a few weeks after my return).
And little about the Nuremberg Trials attracted me. I was
concerned about their charter, particularly that part which
defined an act of aggression as a war crime. That clause
bothered me no end. The Allied powers had all of these
crimes against humanity, and here was an effort to put a
new wrinkle into international law. I thought it was a serious mistake.

Scholars have since questioned both the charter and the
conduct of the Nuremberg Trials. The chief criticism has
centered around the same provision that disturbed me—the
charging of the defendants with planning, initiating, and
waging wars of aggression. The charge was *ex post facto*—
this being a violation not recognized by international law
at the time it was committed. It has also been argued that
to recognize such conduct as a violation of international
law renders every head of state susceptible to such a charge
upon losing a war.

Of course, compromises had to be made at Nuremberg
or the trials would not have been held. Each of the four
countries involved—the United States, Britain, France, and
the Soviet Union—had its own judicial system. The Russians were a continuing problem. They subscribed to the
Judge Roy Bean school of justice: you gave them a trial
and then you hanged them.

At my office one day, I saw a copy of a cablegram sent by
Mr. Justice Jackson to President Harry Truman. In the

cablegram, Justice Jackson advocated that we simply forget about trying to work out our differences with the other powers. We would try those war criminals in our captivity, and the Russians would deal with theirs. Within days, the Russians, knowing that Jackson meant business and not wanting us to withdraw, agreed to sit down and work things out. It could not have been easy, finding a legal blanket that could be spread over the Russians, the French, the British, and the Americans.

In the cases tried in our zone, we encountered no such restraints. The German lawyers were amazed to see their clients receive rights they would not have been granted under their own system of justice.

Soon after V-E Day, I had an occasion to appear at a place code-named the "Ashcan," a secret incarceration point for most of the surviving high officials of the German Reich. The building selected for their confinement was formerly a large resort hotel, with what had been a fine veranda. The grounds were now completely surrounded with barbed wire and in each corner a watchtower was manned by guards armed with machine guns. Day after day, sitting on the veranda in their undershirts were the likes of Göring, Von Ribbentrop, Keitel, Frank, Rosenberg, Jodl.

As I began to walk up the steps to the entrance of the building, the officer in charge of the Ashcan ordered these once powerful men to come to attention. There they stood —disheveled and forlorn, these men responsible for the terrible scenes I had witnessed and the cold-blooded murders I had heard described. I quickly moved on.

6

The Vice-President

❦

For months after the war, I felt frustrated and bored, a condition not uncommon among returning soldiers and retired athletes. I attended my share of dinners, accepted more than my share of plaques, heard the speeches, and made a few of my own. My work on the war crimes trials had attracted notice at home. My name was added to the name of our law firm. It was now Fulbright, Crooker, Freeman, Bates and Jaworski.

We were still a one-car family. I caught a bus to the office so my wife could have the car to take the kids to school. In the twilight, my son, Joe, met me at the bus stop on his bike, and kept me company as I walked home.

Those should have been the halcyon days, and were, except for the gray and restless feeling I could not identify. Perhaps some of it had to do with turning forty. But I had another adjustment to make. The legal world I re-entered after the war had changed. New tax and antitrust laws were being written, amended, argued. International companies, even whole new industries, had emerged. Social and political unrest were around the corner.

My enthusiasm for trying cases was slow to return, but in time it did, for no one reason that I can recall. By the late 1950s I was handling the lawsuit that would bring my firm the largest single fee in its history, up to that time. I negotiated an $8 million settlement in what became known as the Moody estate case. My client was Mrs. Libbie Moody Thompson, the wife of Congressman Clark Thompson, and the daughter of the late William Lewis Moody, Jr., whose business empire—insurance, banks, and hotels—was based in Galveston.

The case lasted three years and was settled in an empty Galveston courtroom, where one could hear the hum of the ceiling fans and a soft Gulf breeze swept the scent of oleander through the open windows. At the request of the Thompsons, our firm had taken the case on a contingent basis. As a result, the fee was $1 million. Although such fees usually went into a pool shared by the senior partners, this one was divided among all the members of the firm.

At that point, representing the wife of Congressman Thompson was as close as I had gotten to politics. My exposure in the Moody case probably did not hurt any when a friend in Austin recommended me to a client I knew by name only. But he was certainly no stranger.

No one can be impartial where Lyndon Baines Johnson is concerned. And no lawyer can be neutral in defense of a client, any more than a vacuum cleaner salesman can come to your door and say, "I would like to tell you the pros and cons of this product."

Lyndon Johnson was my client, my friend, from the winter of 1960 until his death. He had wanted the Democratic nomination for President, started late, and ran hard to catch the front runner, John Fitzgerald Kennedy. As Senate majority leader, Johnson had been a formidable force in Washington. He had pushed through Congress the nation's first civil rights bill in eighty-two years. He had driven the Senate to pass in four hours a Hawaiian statehood bill that had been on the calendar for forty years.

Kennedy himself had introduced him at a dinner in Boston during the early maneuvering: "Some people refer to Senator Johnson as the next President of the United States, but I see no reason why he should take a demotion."

The Democratic national convention could not have denied its nomination to John Kennedy in 1960. He campaigned across the land, and in the primaries, with an energy and skill seldom seen in a political effort.

Kennedy stunned everyone by selecting as his running mate the man who had been his foremost rival. Alone among possible choices, Lyndon Johnson possessed the experience and mettle for the job and at the same time could bring regional balance to the ticket. He helped make the difference in a campaign in which the parties fought to a virtual standoff, and the margin of victory amounted to one vote per precinct.

I had known of Johnson for years, had observed his rise as a young aide to Congressman Dick Kleberg, and had voted for him in each of his campaigns. But as a practicing lawyer, I steered clear of the actual business of politics. Party work, electioneering—these are efforts I willingly leave to others. There are times, however, when the paths of practicing attorney and political candidate cross. The 1960 campaign was such a time for me.

A special emotion and harshness characterize Texas politics. As no one since Sam Houston, the tall, craggy, restless Lyndon Johnson had created his place on the American stage. Texans were proud; many felt a grudging envy of his ascent and power. But this did not mean he was popular. He evoked strange conflicts in people. And no outsider can truly understand the mixture of money, time, and place that lies at the heart of the state's politics; how the party lines are drawn and how they sometimes blur; how Texas can so often reflect the best and the worst of the country's heritage. Here partisanship and high feeling, so acceptable at outdoor rallies and in smoke-filled rooms, carry just as easily into churches and courtrooms—not to confuse one with the other.

The first lawsuit in the 1960 campaign grew out of the fact that the Texas Election Code permitted a candidate to have his name on a general election ballot more than once if he ". . . has been duly nominated for the office of President or Vice-President of the United States and also for an office requiring a statewide vote for election." To help Johnson's chances, the state legislature had advanced the primary from July to May. Thus on May 7, 1960, he was renominated as the party's candidate for the United States Senate. On July 15, 1960, taking the cheers of the crowd beside John F. Kennedy, he was nominated for Vice-President by the Democratic national convention in Los Angeles.

Less than two weeks later, a twenty-four-year-old college student named Michael E. Schwille filed suit in district court in Austin challenging Johnson's right to run for both offices in the November general election. A government major at North Texas State, Schwille was ahead of his time. Political activism on America's campuses would not come into vogue until the mid-1960s. A bit of a rebel, the son of a Democratic precinct judge, he persuaded two lawyers, former FBI agents, to accept the case for a modest fee. Off they went.

Schwille saw the case as a legal crusade. He asked the court to declare unconstitutional a statute passed by the legislature that enabled Johnson to run twice on the same ballot. His complaint charged that voters in the Democratic primary would be deprived of a candidate of their choice in one office or the other. The suit asked that the executive committee of the state party be enjoined from certifying Johnson's name as its nominee for both offices.

Although not directly involved, Texas Republicans had a strong rooting interest in Schwille's case. Since the suit at that point involved a primary election, they had no standing in court. But they were desperate to see Johnson removed from the national ticket. Rumors flew that Schwille was a Republican agent, financed by Republican money. None of the charges were true. He was a true gadfly enjoying his first joust with the political process.

Later, he attended Baylor, my old school. He became a

criminal lawyer, served in the office of the Dallas district attorney, and in 1978 was defeated when he ran for a seat on the district bench—as a Democrat.

I met Schwille only once, during a pretrial hearing in Austin. Afterward he told a friend of mine, "Jaworski walked across the room to shake my hand. He was polite. I could see he was surprised at how young I was. And he looked at me as though I was a pain in the ——. I appreciated how he felt."

The case was no lark, and we had to proceed as though the Republicans were waiting in the wings—which they were. With Johnson's commanding political base in the state, he drew support from a wide range of voters, including some who were quite conservative. On Johnson's appeal to those voters, they felt, the election might very well turn. Many conservative Democrats wanted John Kennedy defeated at all costs. He was Catholic, he was liberal, he was from a state not sympathetic to the oil industry. Given no other distractions, they would be willing to campaign and vote for the Republican candidate, Richard Nixon.

But Senator Johnson's presence as Kennedy's running mate changed the equation. The Democratic ticket figured to draw support in Texas, and across the South, that it would not otherwise have. Sam Rayburn, of Texas, the Speaker of the House for so many years, put the matter in perspective in a heated confrontation with conservative Democrats after the convention. "You can't be Democrats for thirty years," he said, "and for three hundred and sixty-four days, and then vote Republican on the other day."

When the suit was filed to force Johnson to give up one

of his places on the ballot—with the assumption that he would be forced off as candidate for Vice-President—he called and asked that I serve as his chief defense counsel. After obtaining some of the details, I said, "Senator, let me think about it and I'll call you tomorrow with an answer."

There was a long pause on the line and I sensed that he was somewhat taken aback. In later years, when we had become close friends, he often teased me about my hesitation. "Leon, you S.O.B.," he would roar, "any other lawyer in Texas would have taken that case in a minute."

I talked the matter over with my partners. Any time you represent a political figure, there is a potential for controversy. The lawyer, and his firm, may become identified with a candidate, a cause, or an ideology. The reputation of the firm gets involved. It had been a courtesy—I later made it a policy—to review such cases with my partners. With their support, I telephoned the senator the next day and said I would represent him. Other attorneys worked with me, including Ed Clark, of Austin, a Johnson confidant who later became our ambassador to Australia. We had to move quickly. The injunction that was sought could have thrown the entire campaign into chaos if the court granted it.

When the news circulated that I was taking the case, the criticism and denunciation began. Several people called to tell me I was making a grave mistake: my firm could lose clients and have a hard time attracting new ones. Some of the callers were Republicans. Others were Democrats who did not relish the idea of Johnson's running with Kennedy, a liberal, a Catholic, an Easterner not thought to be sympathetic to the oil industry. I ignored them all.

I have been asked if I could accept a case on behalf of someone I did not admire, and with whom I disagreed. The answer is, yes, of course. Lord Erskine, the famed English barrister, said, "It is not our obligation or responsibility to try to pass judgment on the rights of a client. This is the judgment of the court. All we do is give them the protection of the law, and present the client's views—honorably and fairly." If a lawyer selected cases according to his or her own values, most people would never have their day in court.

In district court, we argued that the suit to force Senator Johnson off the ballot did not present a substantial federal question. Since he had not yet been elected to either, he was not attempting to *hold* both offices simultaneously—a clear violation of the U. S. Constitution, since by its terms the offices are mutually exclusive. From that standpoint, the suit was clearly premature. Beyond that, it was also apparent the courts had no jurisdiction.

All the precedents were favorable. Assume that Senator Johnson was re-elected to the Senate and elected to the vice-presidency and *then* sought to hold both offices. If his qualifications to serve in the Senate were challenged, as they would have been, then the Senate, under the Constitution, would decide the issue. If his right to serve as Vice-President was challenged, again as it would have been, then both houses of Congress, acting concurrently, would decide the issue when the Electoral College returns were presented to them.

The suit was smart politics. The strategy seemed obvious. The Republicans had nothing to lose. At the least, they had made a campaign issue out of Johnson's running for two offices. They encouraged the idea that his action was morally questionable, if not illegal. Even if they did not win, the suit had a certain nuisance value. If the case dragged on long enough, it might cast a cloud over the election.

But if his opponents thought they might distract Johnson, or drain off his time by making him fight on more than one front, they were mistaken. He turned over the matter to his attorneys and was hardly heard from again. The only time we talked was when I would give him the results of our latest court test. Lyndon was far too busy campaigning to worry about a lawsuit. He was then on a whistle-stop tour across America. I would pick up the paper in the morning and see which towns he had been in the day before, speaking from the rear platform of his special train. As the train lurched out of the station, he would shout one of the best-remembered lines of his campaign: "What did Richard Nixon ever do for Plant City?"

Meanwhile, Judge Ben Rice granted our motion to dismiss. The other side appealed to the U. S. Supreme Court, which refused to hear the case. Undaunted by those failures, Michael E. Schwille, joined by two others and represented by the same attorneys, brought suit in state court in Dallas. This time they argued that Johnson's name appearing twice on the ballot violated the Texas constitution. Again we went through the same arguments, and again we succeeded in having the suit dismissed.

Now the plaintiffs appealed directly to the Supreme Court of Texas, which held that it did not then have jurisdiction. The proper route for the appeal to travel, the Court said, was through the Court of Civil Appeals, an intermediate court. By then time had run out. They filed their appeal, which was heard on November 7, 1960, the day before the election. We argued and won.

The issues dragged through the courts were not limited to that forum by any means. The press, the public, and, with passion, the Republican candidates joined the debate. Early in the campaign, Johnson met publicly the question of appearing twice on the ballot. He was asked if his dual candidacy did not indicate a lack of confidence in his winning the vice-presidency.

He replied, "No, I don't think so. . . . Members of the House run for the Senate. Members of the Senate come back and run for governor. Governors frequently run for the Senate. In my state, Franklin D. Roosevelt and John Garner were the winningest ticket the Democrats ever had. They carried every state in the Union in 1936 except Maine and Vermont. But Mr. Garner's name was on the ticket because he had a seniority position that was very important to his state. As a matter of fact, his colleagues had elected him Speaker of the House at the same time that he was on the ticket for Vice-President—an identical situation to what you have here."

John Tower was Johnson's opponent in the Senate race. (Afterward, he was elected to fill the vacancy left when Johnson became Vice-President.)

John Kennedy and Lyndon Johnson campaigned hard in

Texas, but especially Johnson. A national candidate worthy
of the name carries his ticket in his own state, and Lyndon
did, by some forty-six thousand votes. This reversed a trend
in Texas, which had been captured by Eisenhower in 1952
and 1956.

The votes Johnson swung in the South elected Jack Kennedy as the country's youngest and first Catholic President.
But the next two years were not to be fulfilling ones for
Lyndon and the disenchantment started immediately. He
was constantly on the move: to Mexico for a brief vaca-
tion. Back to Washington to finish out a short, frustrating
lame-duck session of Congress, as majority leader. Then to
Europe.

As far as I knew, the country had a new government and
the legal nuisances were behind us. I was in Austin having
dinner with Ed Clark at the Headliners' Club when I was
paged to take a phone call. To my surprise, Lyndon Johnson was on the line. The last I had heard, he was in Paris.

I asked where he was.

"Here at home," he said, meaning the ranch at Johnson
City. Then he said, "Leon, I guess you know we've been
enjoined."

I said, "Enjoined? Enjoined from what?"

"On our electoral college votes in Texas. They [the
Republicans] are contesting the election results."

I said, "You mean, without a hearing?"

"That's the information I got."

It was interesting to me how quickly Johnson had
learned of this development. I had heard nothing. But I
blithely said, "Oh well, what you mean is that a suit has

been filed to be set for a hearing, and we'll get a chance to present our case."

Johnson said, "I don't know what you lawyers call it. All I know is we've been enjoined."

He told me that a Republican judge in Houston had issued the order. I knew the judge and had served with him in the Army in Europe. I jotted down Lyndon's phone number and told him I would call back in a few minutes.

I dialed the judge at home. I asked him if a suit had been filed in his court involving Lyndon Johnson.

"Yes."

"What did you do, set it down for a hearing or something?"

"I am not going to hear it myself."

"Did you take any interim action?"

"Yes. I granted a restraining order."

I swallowed hard. "Judge, you don't have any more jurisdiction on that than a justice of the peace." Quite simply, the proper forum for such a contest was the Senate itself.

"Well," he countered, "I'm not going to hear it. Another judge will."

I said, "All the same, I find this very disconcerting." I called Lyndon back, then returned to the table, pulled up the chair loudly, and broke the news to Ed Clark.

The Republicans had charged that irregularities had taken place at the polls, and they had asked the state canvassing board to order a recount of the ballots. Pending a hearing in district court, the Democratic electors could not be certified.

A similar action was taking place in Illinois. Between

them, the two states controlled enough votes to overturn the election. In four days, the Electoral College was to convene for the purpose of confirming John Kennedy and Lyndon Johnson as the country's new leadership. There was no time to waste. I hurried back to Houston and met the next morning, a Friday, in the judge's chambers. Given the urgency of the moment, I made little attempt to be diplomatic. I told the judge, and the attorneys for the other side, that I was going to file a motion to dismiss the suit and I wanted it heard as soon as possible. I made clear my position that this court had no authority in the matter. The hearing was set for Monday.

As I started to leave his chambers, the judge said, softly, "Leon, do you have a moment?"

As I walked toward him, he said, quietly, "You're going to have to convince me that I don't have jurisdiction in this case."

Well, the rule was clear. In an election dispute of this kind, the Senate alone had the authority to determine the outcome. This is why, in legal terms, we say the courts have no jurisdiction. But the judge, in his wisdom, went further. Although now convinced he had no jurisdiction, he gave the other side an opportunity to show the type of irregularities listed in the complaint.

As the judge began to wade through the documents, I noticed his eyebrows arching higher and higher. He was a shrewd jurist who did not squander time. He looked up and asked, "Is this it? Is this all you have?" The affidavits were based on hearsay, and on minor and insignificant errors without any showing as to whether they were hurtful to voting Democrats or voting Republicans. Even if the court had taken jurisdiction, it would have had to find against the complainant on the claims of irregularity. The suit was dismissed.

I went to bed that night, bone-weary, having worked nearly around the clock over the weekend to prepare my arguments for Monday. I had been asleep an hour or so when the phone rang. In a whispery, conspiratorial voice, Lyndon Johnson said, "I just want you to know that I got a report that you were absolutely FABULOUS today. SUPERB. I heard there had never been an argument made in court as illustrious as yours."

Understatement was never one of Lyndon's strong suits. He was like a St. Bernard whose kisses would leave the side of your face raw. But his gratitude was genuine. After I thanked him for his compliments, he said, his voice now brisk, "Leon, what is it I can do?"

I said, "My friend, I can think of only one thing. Run up to Washington as soon as you can and get yourself inaugurated."

Not many hours later, the Democratic electors met in Texas. All the legal road blocks had been pulled aside, and the electors certified that a majority of the voters of the state had cast their ballots for John F. Kennedy and Lyndon B. Johnson.

Between the two men, I believe, there was respect and friendship. For a fact, I know Lyndon felt a fondness for Jack Kennedy, his grace, his humor, his kindness. Of course, he was amused, and sometimes puzzled, by people's fascination with Kennedy's style and potential, when his own accomplishments, his unique skill at connecting the right Washington wires, so often seemed to go unappreciated. But he certainly did not blame John Kennedy for being charming.

No one gave Johnson much credit for idealism, but he cared about people, believed in their essential goodness, and passed more social legislation on their behalf than any President of this century. He lacked glamour, but he could walk into a room and dominate it instantly. He had a boundless capacity for hard work, the only man I ever knew who had no hobbies and wanted none, who was truly comfortable only when talking, thinking, or doing politics.

A few weeks after the election I was invited to the White House, along with lawyers from other parts of the country, in support of the civil rights effort. During a long meeting in the Blue Room, both John and Robert Kennedy spoke and, finally, Lyndon Johnson. Curiously, Johnson was the star. His speech captivated his audience. Given the right room and the right crowd, he was unequaled. His language soared. He spoke as a man resented by some of his fellow Southerners for demanding equal rights for blacks, and not fully trusted by some blacks for being southern. He recalled how he had asked the governor of his own state, John Connally, "How we can justify having a sign on the rest room doors in the Capitol that say, 'For Whites Only'? The next day," he went on, "the governor of Texas had those signs removed."

Lyndon had a talent for reducing monumental problems to their most basic points. After his talk, the lawyers, these sophisticated leaders of the Bar, applauded and crowded around him, all but ignoring the President and the Attorney General. It was hard for me to understand how Johnson could be so persuasive and moving at such moments, and on other occasions deliver a speech so flat and toneless that people would drop off to sleep as though they had been drugged.

That evening, Lyndon was the host at a poolside party at The Elms, the home he had purchased from Pearl Mesta. He was in one of his euphoric moods, open and playful. As the party got going, I saw him reach into a bowl of smoked oysters and scoop out a huge handful. As he did, Lady Bird came down on his wrist with a karate chop and he dropped them all. She snapped, "Lyndon, you just know those things are loaded with oil!" After his heart attack in the mid-1950s, Lady Bird kept a strict watch on his diet.

Lyndon was a man of extra dimensions, who thought bigger, laughed louder, and got mad faster than most men. He had the ability to put his anger to work for him, to make people move, jump, change their minds. No one was immune. I experienced the blowtorch of Johnson's temper some months before the end of his troubled presidency. He had appointed me to his Commission on Violence, chaired by Milton Eisenhower, the younger brother of Ike. I had not taken any permanent position in Washington, and Lyndon's way of getting back at me was to put me on every government commission that came along.

We reached a point in the commission's work where no funding was available. Lloyd Cutler, a Washington attorney, acting as our executive director, went to Joe Califano, then an assistant to the President, and reported that the members were frustrated. Unless money was forthcoming to get the job done, Califano was told, there would be some resignations.

That night, my wife, Jeannette, and I had been invited to a dinner at the White House along with five or six other couples. The men had collected in one room, where cocktails were being served, while the women visited in another room. When the President walked in he said hello, seemed friendly, and moved on to greet his other guests. Then he came back to me and said, "I just read that goddamn memorandum from Califano."

I looked at him blankly. "I don't know what you're talking about."

He said, "Well, you ought to know." He grabbed me by the lapels—one of his occasional habits—and snapped, "I want you to march every one of those S.O.B.s into my office tomorrow morning and I'm going to fire every one of them."

As politely as I could, I disengaged his hands from my lapels and muttered, "Mr. President, I am at a complete loss. I have no idea what you are talking about."

He said, "Dammit to hell, I'm not going to put up with that kind of guff." He poked his finger in my chest. I believe if he had found a soft spot it would have gone right through. He was giving me the complete treatment and, finally, I said, "Now, wait a minute. At least let me catch up with you."

With that he motioned to an aide, sent him down to the Oval Office, and had him bring back Califano's memorandum, which I read and found somewhat pointed. But I suspected Joe had done so deliberately to rivet the President's attention. Califano was sympathetic to social causes and became the Secretary of Health, Education, and Welfare under Carter. He had told me before, "You can't get any money out of Johnson unless you put some real heat on him." His report had the commission on the verge of a mutiny.

I handed the memo back and said, "Mr. President, I am not a party to this."

He sort of slapped the report out of my hand, like an officer inspecting a soldier's rifle, and handed it to his aide. Nothing more was said, and silently we walked into the dining room to take our seats.

I had mixed feelings as I picked at my food. I kept smoothing my lapels, as if his thumbprints were still visible. His gesture had startled me, but I was not offended. As Hubert Humphrey once said, "He could take a bite out of you bigger than a T-bone steak, and the very next day he would put his arms around you like a long-lost brother. I sometimes tried to stir up a little trouble just so I could be loved up once again."

After dinner he made one of his "My dear friends" speeches, warm and touching. When he finished, and the dishes were being cleared, I walked outside and he followed me. It was obvious he wanted to soften the impression he had left earlier. "Say, who is this associate counsel on your committee?" he asked.

I said I didn't know.

He frowned, trying to remember. "Oh, he's connected with some big New York law firm."

That line of conversation would lead nowhere. Lyndon was not very good at small talk. So I looked him in the eye and said, "Tell me, Mr. President, do you think I would do anything to embarrass you? Or let you down?"

He said, "Aw, no, Leon, I know you better than that."

I said, "Then, please, don't ever infer it, again. Okay?"

He ducked his head and said, "Well, I didn't mean to infer it."

Johnson could work himself into a fit over the most minor of problems, as well as slights, real and imagined. But he was contrite in proportion to how much time and volume had gone into his tantrum, and how chagrined he felt later. Though his anger may have been directed elsewhere, he often vented his feelings on the hapless soul nearest at hand. He was often surprised that anyone would take these outbursts personally. He would tell a story to illustrate his point.

A friend of his named Otto once went to a high school dance at Albert, after drinking too much beer. The first thing he did was walk in and announce to the entire dance hall that he could "lick any Dutch knucklehead in the house."

At that, a great big German farm boy with muscles like boulders grabbed Otto by his shirt collar and said, "Vot you say?"

"I can whip any Dutch knucklehead in the house," Otto repeated. "Are you a Dutch knucklehead?"

"I'm not any kind of a knucklehead," the farm boy said.

"Well then," said Otto, "I wasn't talking about you."

Later, on that night of the crushed lapels, I thought I

saw his emotions laid as bare as they ever were. He was alternately reflective, somber, uncertain, teasing. We were in the sitting quarters upstairs, with our wives, when he suddenly turned to Jeannette and said, "One of my regrets about leaving office is the fact that I was never able to put Leon on the Supreme Court." He paused, for effect, then added, "but he always told me he wanted to be a big-shot lawyer in Houston."

Startled, Jeannette turned to me and said, "Did you tell the President that?"

I said, "You just heard the President speak, didn't you?" I was not going to argue, if I could avoid it, with Lyndon Johnson.

It no longer matters whether Johnson meant to offer me a seat on the high court, or to appoint me to the job of Attorney General, as some have suggested. The Supreme Court is supposed to be every lawyer's dream. But it was never mine. One night by the White House pool, in mid-December, a few days after the Kennedy assassination, he seemed to be offering me carte blanche. I was then working with the Warren Commission, at the Texas end of the investigation. We were not alone, and the President said, "Okay, Leon. You have been doing things for me. Now it's my turn to do something for you. What do you want?"

He was a man who believed in the quid pro quo. He looked at me, disbelieving, when I said, "I don't want anything. No job. No favors. Nothing."

No one spoke. Finally, Johnson, who was in the pool, hanging on to the side, splashed a little water with his hand and said, "Okay. In that case, I'll just send you a Christmas card."

I was not attracted to Washington, or to the idea of being glued to a desk or a bench. And, frankly, I valued my independence too much to limit it by accepting a federal appointment.

He was not an easy man to refuse, as anyone who came into his orbit knew. Once, when Everett Dirksen was the minority leader of the House, Johnson invited him to the Oval Office. He needed Dirksen's support on a crucial vote, but the craggy Illinois Republican was resisting. The President had placed an early issue of the *Congressional Record* on the coffee table between them, opened to a page containing Dirksen's maiden speech on the floor of the House in 1933.

The President said, "Ev, you remember this? A lot of people have forgotten this speech, but I just happened to run across it the other day."

Dirksen knew at a glance what it was. By the standards of the 1960s it could be considered offensive to blacks—and this was at a time when Dirksen was enjoying a new popularity among the blacks because of his support of the 1965 Civil Rights Bill.

As Johnson described the scene: "He looked at me solemnly, those eyebrows went up, and those big tones just rolled out across the room. 'Mr. President!' he said. 'That's blackmail!' I said, 'Now, Ev, you know nobody's going to see that. Now let's go back over this thing. I want to know what I can do to relieve you of your doubts so we can get your vote.' He didn't bat an eye. He said, 'Mr. President, you know I always stand ready to support my President any way I can.'"

He was, of course, a man of paradoxes, one who wanted to do things for people out of a generous spirit, but who thought every person had a price; a man who wanted to be understood, but loved to create mystery; whose vision for the country was large and grand, even as he fretted that no one would remember his good works or honor his best efforts.

Vietnam was his albatross. Johnson believed that the war had to be fought, that the sacrifices had to be made. Certainly he felt that way until the final months of his presidency. One has to remember what the climate was when he took office. Two Presidents before him had made commitments in Southeast Asia. We were not yet to the end of that era when the popular opinion was that America had to confront godless communism at every turn. According to the polls, 67 per cent of the people supported our involvement in Vietnam as late as 1965.

I sat in his bedroom one night, around 11 P.M., while he buried himself in a folder marked "Vietnam," a sheaf of papers as thick as the Detroit telephone directory. It contained intelligence reports, casualty lists, private communications from our ambassadors and generals and from foreign embassies. He seemed lost in the painful thoughts those papers inspired, and two or three times I tried to slip out the door. Each time, without looking up, he would say, "Don't leave, Leon. Stay a little longer and talk to me."

But we didn't talk. I would just sit there, watching the grief etched so clearly in his face. He had increased the American role in a war that he thought was right, one that had torn and divided and savaged the country. Patriotism and liberty were not products to be bartered, he thought. He had not wavered in his belief that the Vietnamese needed our aid and the troops we sent deserved our loyalty. But when the war refused to end, when it seemed to become a bottomless pit, he must have been consumed by the one unthinkable thought: What if it was all in vain?

Finally, I said, "You have things to do. Let me tell you good-night."

When I walked into the corridor, my wife and Lady Bird were waiting. I asked Mrs. Johnson how late he stayed up. She glanced at her watch and said, "He's just starting now. He'll read for two hours, maybe more. He'll read every report from Vietnam."

I shook my head and turned to go back into his room, not really knowing why. Lady Bird touched my arm and said, "Don't, Leon. Just let him be. He needs to do it. He can't go to sleep without reading them."

Johnson had a way of reaching out to a friend at hand, to air his problems and confide his doubts. The Vietnam War weighed heavily on him. He was acutely conscious that it had kept his presidency from achieving what his own best hopes had been.

He could easily plunge himself, and those around him, into gloom, and if I could I tried to take the edge off those conversations, even though I never underestimated his personal torment. He said to me one day, "I wonder if you have any idea what the President and his family have to endure?"

I said I could only guess.

"Do you know," he persisted, "how many threats we

have received here on my life, or the lives of my family? Over twelve thousand."

Before I could reply, we both became aware of a man working on a power line a distance away from us. Lyndon nodded and said, "Leon, you see that man over there? He could have a gun and be shooting in our direction at any moment."

I coughed and said, "Uh, Mr. President, would you mind moving over a little bit?"

But Johnson had a fine sense of history. I once spent three hours in the Rose Garden with him, totally engrossed, as he spoke of the government, how it functioned, the men and women who made it work, what was needed to improve the system. He said he believed that the time had come when there should be two Vice-Presidents, one an executive assistant to the President, a sort of business manager, who would be concerned with those regulations and resolutions and requests from Congress that consume so much of the President's time. This office would be an appointive rather than an elected post, so that ability would be the only consideration, and not the political needs of balancing a ticket or healing a party.

Johnson realized sooner than most that his presidency would not be a tranquil one, and that many of his goals and ideas would not be implemented in his lifetime. He surely did not inspire the kind of following of either John or Robert Kennedy. Finesse was not his style. Where some people snip at life with a manicure scissors, Lyndon used a cleaver.

7

The Governor

The large Houston law firms in the early 1960s, and those in many other parts of the land, were like country clubs— meaning no Jews or blacks; membership by invitation only.

Our firm would later take the lead in changing those policies. But at the time we told ourselves, as many people did, that traditions die slowly; we were a product of that society, we had not created it. There were no black generals or senators or Supreme Court justices.

In retrospect, it may sound hollow to say, but we *tried* to exert some moral leadership. The partners encouraged the performance of *pro bono* work, and I attempted to do my share. I learned as a boy in Waco that the smart farmer puts something back into the ground after he harvests his crops.

During my year as president of the Texas Bar Association, in 1961, an article of mine appeared in the law journal of the ABA entitled "The Unpopular Cause." In it I appealed to my colleagues not to shrink from cases, or situations, that were controversial. Soon enough, I was in a position to practice what I had preached. The Justice Department asked me to prosecute Ross Barnett, the governor of Mississippi, for defying a court order to let blacks enroll at Ole Miss.

When historians tell the story of our time, they will discover a central truth about this generation. It has been shaped by the wrenching, divisive, yet creative attempt we are making to ensure equal rights for *all* Americans.

The effort has not been an easy one. Solving massive social problems never is. Yet we are trying. Fundamental to the success of this campaign is our system of law. If Americans can maintain their traditional respect for the law, as that system sets standards that are equitable and just, then there is hope.

Generally, we have done so. Court decisions have moved slowly but steadily in the direction of guaranteeing equality before the law for all our citizens.

It has not been a serene and steady process. Defiance and violence are more visible and better remembered than progress, which is often quiet and matter-of-fact. There has been inexcusable ugliness, and doubtless there will be more. But like storms at sea, sporadic acts of violence do not necessarily mean that the voyage of understanding and harmony will not be completed.

We stand too close to the vast issue of racial justice to judge all of these incidents accurately. Yet because of their high drama, and the determination of the opposing forces, certain key encounters stand out. I was involved in one of them.

In September of 1962, a federal court ordered the University of Mississippi to admit its first black student, a twenty-nine-year-old Air Force veteran named James H. Meredith. Until the state tried to block his enrollment, and his name became familiar in print and on the air, I had never heard of Meredith. Few people had.

A more dangerous issue than the social implications of the Meredith case was at stake. Put simply, it was: Can a state, or a public official, or a mob, defy the authority of the United States of America? Is the federal government indeed sovereign and paramount, or can the orders of its courts be ignored and the authority to enforce them resisted? In this context, the Meredith case went far beyond the issue of integration versus segregation. It reached to the very soul of our system and, indeed, brought into question whether we had a government at all.

By the time I was brought into the case, Meredith had been admitted to classes and Ole Miss was technically an integrated school. That is, his experience had demonstrated that the U. S. Army, in sufficient force, could make sure that a black student could attend his state university.

So that issue had been resolved. The other had not. To understand this aspect of the case, we must recall briefly what had happened.

Meredith's right to attend the University of Mississippi had been thoroughly litigated. His case had been heard in district court, in the Court of Appeals, and then by the Supreme Court. All the arguments had been made, all the legal remedies exhausted. Finally came the end of the road. The Fifth Circuit ordered that Meredith be admitted and that no one, including authorities of the school or the state government itself, could interfere.

In a scathing majority opinion, written by Judge John Minor Wisdom, the Fifth Circuit reversed the lower court. In denying Meredith's admission, the district judge had found "as a fact, that the University is not a racially segregated institution." He quoted the testimony of the trustees that the question of race had never been discussed at any meeting of the board. He concluded that although segregation was the custom before 1954—and the Supreme Court's landmark ruling in *Brown* v. *Board of Education*—"there is no custom or policy now, nor was there any at the time of the plaintiff's application, which excluded Negroes from entering the University." There were blacks on the Ole Miss campus. They worked as custodians and as kitchen help.

Judge Wisdom noted: "This about-face in policy, news of which may startle some people in Mississippi, could have been accomplished only by telepathic communication among the University's administrators. . . . It seemed to us that 'what everybody knows the court must know.' "

Bitter-end segregationists in the state had vowed to resist the integration of the university, whatever the cost. Their champion was to be Ross Barnett, the governor, who had been elected to office on the strength of a relentlessly racist campaign. Many Southerners of that sad era were not above playing politics with so emotional an issue. But what Barnett said seemed to rise from the depths of his feelings.

In one speech he had declared, "The Negro is different because God made him different to punish him. His forehead slants back. His nose is different. His lips are different. And his color is sure different."

Whether out of conviction, or because he recognized a popular cause, the governor moved to block the registration of Meredith. His actions, he insisted, were solidly based on the Tenth Amendment: "The powers not delegated to the United States by the Constitution, nor prohibited by it to the States, are reserved to the States respectively, or to the people." Those reserved powers, the argument ran, include the authority to preserve order and protect public safety. Barnett claimed that the interests of order and safety required him to "interpose and invoke the police powers of the state."

But this was a constitutionally footless line of argument. The old states' rights doctrine that a state can interpose its authority to void a federal law within its own borders was struck down long ago—pragmatically by the Civil War and legally by decisions of the U. S. Supreme Court. In 1932 Chief Justice Charles Evans Hughes, speaking for a unanimous court, declared it to be "manifest" that a state governor could not invoke his powers to infringe anyone's rights under the Constitution. In the Little Rock decision in 1958 the Supreme Court handed down a unanimous opinion that the school desegregation order "can neither be nullified openly and directly by state legislators or state executives or judicial officers, nor nullified indirectly by them through evasive schemes."

There was only one way for Governor Barnett to prevent

Meredith's enrollment without coming into head-on conflict with the federal government. He could shut down the university. But the students at Ole Miss, with their futures at stake, wanted it to stay open. So did their parents. So did the townspeople of Oxford, who depended on the school for economic survival. So did many Mississippians who had never set foot on the campus, but who followed the fortunes of its football team with passion. As long as the university remained open to other Mississippians, it remained open, by order of the federal courts, to James H. Meredith.

So emotion replaced reason, and the stage was set for what could have become an open rebellion. As events neared a climax, the extremists had their hour. In many a white Mississippian's heart the historic cry of interposition and near-secession struck a responsive chord.

With each rejection of Meredith by Barnett and his lieutenant governor, Paul Johnson, more Mississippians deluded themselves that their defiance was going to be a turning point in the battle for states' rights against the unchecked might of the central government.

On the one hand, Barnett incited them by making defiant statements, and by allowing his authority and responsibility as governor to become a pawn in a situation that was rapidly getting out of control. On the other, he resigned himself in his own mind to the inevitability of Meredith's admission. He indicated as much in his private conversations with the President and the Attorney General. He was a man bargaining to save face, to salvage what he could of "our way of life."

His dilemma was also theirs. The Kennedys could not let Barnett get away with persisting in his defiance; that would have invited such challenges from all over the South, subverting not only justice but the entire federal system. But the use of armed force against a state can also damage the federal system. And, as practical Democrats, the Kennedys had to reflect upon the prospect that military intervention in Mississippi might be politically disastrous to the party in the South.

They were willing to do all in their power to skirt the edge of violence that threatened to erupt, and to work with Barnett as long as the uncompromisable point—Meredith's admission to the university—was not touched.

Meredith had applied to Ole Miss only a few days after President Kennedy was inaugurated. The election of 1960 was the first time that civil rights had been a major issue with both parties. The Democrats had adopted the stronger platform. Meredith was on record as saying that if Richard Nixon had been elected, he might not have applied.

By blocking Meredith's admission, in open defiance of a court order, Barnett chose a collision course. Throughout our history such conflicts have been rare, if only because it is so obvious that in a showdown of strength the federal government must prevail. Except for three Confederate governors arrested after the Civil War, only one incumbent state governor—Warren Terry McCray, of Indiana, in 1924—has ever been sentenced to imprisonment under federal law. He was convicted of misuse of the mails, a felony that had nothing to do with a conflict of federal and state powers. No state governor had ever been sentenced for contempt of a federal court. Arkansas' Orval Faubus made an ugly mess in Little Rock in 1957, but he did not defy any specific court order. As soon as President Eisenhower sent in the troops he scuttled off to the sidelines.

Three times Meredith was turned away from the Ole Miss campus. After the first episode, Governor Barnett was scheduled to appear before the Court of Appeals in New Orleans to answer charges of civil contempt. As expected, he stayed in Mississippi. The court tried him *in absentia*, found him guilty, gave him four days to "purge himself" of the contempt, and set a stern penalty if he failed to comply· a fine of $10,000 a day and confinement in the custody of the U. S. Attorney General.

Once cited, Barnett could have purged himself easily. All he had to do was return to the fold and do as he had been ordered. Instead he continued to defy the court, which went to an unusual length to bring him into line. It asked the Attorney General to prosecute him for *criminal* contempt. Thus the court alleged that his conduct was not only flagrant and serious—two died and hundreds were injured in the riots that resulted at Ole Miss—but willfully done.

At this point I entered the case. The decision had been made at the Department of Justice to bring in outside counsel. It appeared likely that Robert Kennedy would have to testify to certain telephone conversations he had had with Ross Barnett. Kennedy, and the men directly under him, could hardly prosecute a case in which they might be witnesses.

Nicholas Katzenbach, then the deputy attorney general, called me and asked if I would help prosecute the governor of Mississippi. I had been recommended, he said, by prominent members of the American Bar Association and approved by Elbert Tuttle, the chief judge for the Court of Appeals of the Fifth Circuit. Katzenbach had been watching the Ole Miss developments from the early stages, and had personally assured Meredith that U.S. marshals would accompany him when he attempted to enroll. I knew Nick well and admired him. He was a calm, thoughtful lawyer and an honorable man. We had worked together when I was a member of the ABA's committee on the federal judiciary, which investigates the qualifications of judges proposed for federal appointments.

One of the judges I had screened was Griffin B. Bell, of Georgia, before his assignment to the Fifth Circuit. We had never met. But my duties required that I poke into every nook and corner of his life, in a procedure not unlike an FBI screening. I roamed across the state, talking to lawyers and judges who had worked with and around Griffin Bell. They talked about his integrity and fortitude. He had helped draft the school integration plan in Georgia, one that went too far to suit the whites and not far enough to please the blacks. He was a moderate, at a time when moderation was not in fashion.

My report was a favorable one. Fourteen years later, I testified on his behalf when Bell's nomination as Attorney General under President Carter was at issue. No one in recent memory had been more qualified for that office. His rulings in later civil rights cases had been marked by fairness and sensitivity.

So I did not need a scorecard to know the players when I flew to Washington, that November day in 1962, to meet with Robert Kennedy; Katzenbach; Burke Marshall, then the chief of the Civil Rights Division in the Department of Justice; and his successor, John Doar.

We were sitting in the anteroom, waiting for the Attorney General to finish a conversation, when Jacqueline Kennedy appeared. She had dropped by to inspect the crayon pictures that Bobby's younger children had drawn, which were now pinned all over his office walls. The drawings provided an oddly charming background to the somber business at hand.

Although I had met the President several times, this was my first exposure to Bobby. For all their physical resemblance—the eyes, the voice, the mannerisms—I was struck by how different they were. John Kennedy had an enormous self-assurance. There was a tautness to Bobby that you sensed immediately. Yet his instincts seemed quick and sharp and he was able to cut to the heart of an issue. Of course, I had no way of judging his legal ability. When the President appointed him as Attorney General, he had joked that Bobby needed the experience before he went into private practice.

Our meeting went well. We talked about the unique problems posed by the situation in Mississippi, a state of small towns and cities. The capital, Jackson, was a city of 150,000 people, three times the size of the next largest community. Thus **there** was no Atlanta or New Orleans or

Dallas or Nashville, where some white liberal sentiment could be tapped for support. The state was solidly behind the stand of Ross Barnett, a man the federal government was now asking me to prosecute.

An editorial in the Meridian *Star* expressed the prevailing mood in Mississippi:

> . . . Some misguided people ask what difference it makes if only a few Negroes go to a white school. The difference is that the first Negro is only the opening wedge for a flood in time to come.
>
> Integrationists, according to their own statements, will never be satisfied with "token integration." Massive integration will mean future intermarriage. Intermarriage in the South, where we are so evenly divided white and colored, means the end of both races as such, and the emergence of a tribe of mongrels.
>
> We must lock shields. We must fight for our race and for the South to the last bitter ditch. We must never lose heart.

I returned to Texas to think matters over. I had no illusions about the case. The main drama had been played out. Still, someone has to sweep up after the audience leaves. I promptly told the Attorney General's office that I was available. I was asked to keep the matter in confidence until an announcement could be made in Washington.

It is hard for many to understand today the forces that descended on southern moderates fifteen or twenty years ago. There were those who felt the South should be dragged into the twentieth century, even if kicking and screaming. There were others who simply urged obedience to the law. Neither course was popular. Not only the bigots opposed racial integration. Many did whose attitudes had been shaped by time and history, and who simply resisted what they regarded as outside pressure, even though they knew the goal was just.

At the time I was brought into the case, I was serving as president of the State Bar of Texas. I anticipated that some members would not approve of my acting as a prosecutor for the Kennedys, and I debated with myself whether I should resign my office. Then I thought more carefully. If I resigned, it might be interpreted as a tacit admission that the prosecution of Barnett was not consistent with the views of the Texas Bar.

Although not a part of the cotton South, Texas had the same roots. The last shots of the Civil War were fired there. It has been said of the South, as was once said of the Bourbons in France, that we never forget the past and never learn from it. I wanted to believe that judgment was wrong.

The idea that a person can choose which laws or court orders to obey, and which to defy, is dangerous, even poisonous, to our system of government. To say that, if one's conscience speaks to the contrary, one is justified in ignoring the law is the same as saying that the rule of law is not to be the yardstick of our society's conduct. If a civil rights leader disobeys a law because it offends his moral belief of what is right, then will a segregationist not feel free to do the same? And if an exception is tolerated, where is the line drawn? A conscientious objector to the income tax, for example, might find such a philosophy quite appealing. The inevitable result would be to weaken the foundation on which our system of law and order rests. This reasoning was an important consideration to accept the task that had been urged upon me.

Robert Kennedy announced my appointment sooner than he intended because rumors had begun to leak out. It came on a Saturday morning, the first week in December. Both of Houston's afternoon papers carried the story with banner headlines in their early editions. I had been at my office briefly, but went home at noon because I was to attend a football game in the afternoon. By then, television and radio stations were also carrying the news and the phone rang constantly. Calls poured in from supposed friends, from strangers, and from cranks. The so-called friends wailed in anguish. Strangers denounced me, the cranks threatened. At the football game there were icy stares from people sitting around us, and a few simply looked away.

That evening my wife and I went to a party given by one of Houston's most prominent citizens. Our hosts were friendly, but many guests found it convenient not to notice us. Later, as we waited for an attendant to bring our car, an oilman sidled up to me and said, "Leon, I have known you for over twenty-five years. Tonight is the first criticism I have ever heard of you, and it was sharp." That night, although we had not asked for it, police put guards around our home.

In the days afterward, there were many bitter and angry letters. I threw all the anonymous mail into the trash basket, but I answered those from friends who seemed genuinely disturbed.

A society matron, a patron of the arts, wrote that she

was "distressed" to learn that I would prosecute Barnett.
She said she "could not bear to see one of whom I am so
fond, fall in my estimation." Then she exhorted me "not
to be a cat's paw to try to silence the eloquent voice of the
fine old South." Then the final thrust: "Many of your
friends and admirers are heart and soul for Barnett and believe what he is standing for far transcends any law of any
court."

From the president of a mortgage and trust company in
a nearby city came a letter with these accolades: "Every
mentally mature person knows that you are participating in
the Mississippi affair to curry favor with the Administration and, probably, at the instructions of your bishop. I
hope your daughter has a nigger baby."

The man was a stranger to me but he had signed his
name. For a brief, heated moment I thought about driving
out to his office and breaking his nose. But I could understand these emotional reactions from laymen. I was more
deeply troubled by the attitude of many lawyers, who
blandly asserted that a Southerner who took part in the
contempt proceedings was not only committing treason
against the traditions of the South, but was wronging a
"noble" governor.

Skeptics and critics were busy. A judge, a friend, took me
aside at a Bar meeting and asked, pointedly, "What is it—
the Supreme Court?" I told him I was surprised and disappointed that he should ask such a question. Then he said,
"Well, you have been hurt and badly hurt by accepting."
Even judges were unwilling to give a Texas lawyer credit

for performing a duty, unless there was a quid pro quo. Such was the racial climate of the early 1960s.

The state legislature was to convene within a few weeks, and I learned that a senator planned to offer a resolution censuring me for serving as government counsel. He boasted that it would be the first resolution dropped into the hopper for 1963. Friends of mine persuaded the senator not to present his resolution. But the criticism continued.

I received many letters from lawyers, many intemperate, some nasty, calling on me to resign as president of the State Bar. The Bar's chairman of the board polled the directors, and by a majority vote it was decided that no statements should be offered; the matter should be regarded as personal.

Not all of the letters were negative, of course. Many commended me. But I was anguished to find that so many attorneys, and our more sophisticated citizens, failed to understand that Governor Barnett's acts struck directly at the supremacy of law. Whether he was guilty of criminal contempt was not the issue at the moment. That would be determined later. The issue was the direction by a high court, the second highest in the land, that Barnett be charged and tried. Whether an issue is popular or unpopular, lawyers, as officers of the court, must be ready to do their duty as advocates.

In the criticism that flowed, I saw the specters of prejudice and hate. They blotted out sound reason and, in some instances, pushed protests and castigations beyond the limits of decency. Some of my firm's clients protested, too.

To one, our senior partner, John H. Crooker, Sr. (now dead), wrote a letter that was a model of restraint and reason:

> Your recent letter has just reached me and I hasten to acknowledge its receipt. Having been born in Alabama of Southern parents and reared in Houston, I have a thoroughly sympathetic understanding of what is called the "racial question." Having engaged in the active practice of law for well over a half of a century, I have strong convictions as to the duties of all citizens and especially lawyers to respect and uphold decrees and judgments of our duly and regularly constituted courts—even though I may not agree with all terms and provisions of every such decree and judgment. It seems plain and clear that if citizens should be accorded the privilege of obeying *only* such Court decrees and judgments as might have their full approval, we would no longer have a government of law, and the result might easily lead to chaos and anarchy.
>
> To put the matter another way: The sole and only issue before the Circuit Court of Appeals (incidentally, composed entirely of Southern judges including two Houstonians) is whether or not its decrees and judgments are to be obeyed—or whether they may be disobeyed by flagrant mob violence. I may add that it would be a sad day if lawyers—who are especially obliged to uphold decrees and judgments of courts—were to be timid and unwilling to support the courts merely because their decrees and judgments might be unpopular. And, certainly, this would be true, even if some of our very best citizens might be displeased with such decrees and judgments.

It was crucial to understand how Governor Barnett's conduct had brought him into conflict with the court during those tense days and hours when due process of law was menaced by rabble and zealots alike. The confrontation began when Barnett blocked the path of James

Meredith as he attempted to register at the University of Mississippi campus at Oxford—the first of three encounters.

A few days later, the Court of Appeals of the Fifth Circuit entered a temporary restraining order enjoining the governor from interfering with the admission of Meredith to the university. That same afternoon, John Doar and James McShane, the chief U.S. marshal, led Meredith to Room 1007, the office of the state college board, in the Capitol building at Jackson.

John Doar had been a successful small-town lawyer, and a Republican, when President Eisenhower appointed him to the Civil Rights Division. He proved his bravery many times. When a demonstration threatened to turn violent after the funeral in Jackson of Medgar Evers, the slain civil rights leader, Doar stepped between the police guns and a crowd of angry blacks armed with rocks and Coke bottles and restored order. Our paths would cross again during the Watergate case, when Doar served as general counsel to the House Judiciary Committee. He is now a partner in a prominent New York law firm.

Doar is tall, reserved, self-assured. He and McShane must have made an interesting pair. The marshal was ruddy-faced, muscular, a former New York policeman and a onetime Golden Gloves boxing champion. Meredith had two good men running interference for him.

As they reached the door it swung open with a timing that was theatrical. There stood Governor Ross Barnett, beefy, graying, frosty-eyed behind thick glasses. A crowd of people, including newsmen, troopers, and TV cameramen, pushed and shoved as Doar said, calmly, "Governor Barnett, I'm John Doar of the Justice Department. . . . I'm here to present you with these papers and to get on with the business of registering Mr. Meredith."

Barnett's reply was to draw a typewritten sheet from a pocket and read off a "proclamation" addressed to Meredith. To "preserve the peace, dignity and tranquillity" of the state, he intoned, "I hereby finally deny you admission to the University of Mississippi."

Doar and McShane escorted Meredith back to their car, past a gauntlet of jeering, gleeful spectators.

The next day came the third attempt to register Meredith, returning again to Oxford. Barnett had planned to be there, but his plane was grounded by bad weather. He sped to the scene by car, but did not arrive until after the encounter. In his absence, the man blocking the way was Paul Johnson, the lieutenant governor. He stood in the middle of the roadway at the main entrance of the campus, with about twenty state troopers backing him up. About one hundred feet behind them, a dozen Mississippi sheriffs stood in a single rank across the road. Behind them, forming a third line of defense, three police cars were parked end to end.

In the meantime, negotiations were taking place behind the scenes, including phone calls between the Kennedys and Ross Barnett. Some of the conversations were recorded. In one, the President appeared to be conciliatory.

"Here's my problem," he began. "I don't know Mr. Meredith and I didn't put him in the university, but on the other hand under the Constitution I have to carry out the orders of the court. I don't want to do it in any way that causes difficulty to you or anyone else, but I've got to do it."

The President's main concern was to avoid bloodshed. He asked Barnett if he could maintain law and order during Meredith's integration of Ole Miss. The governor replied, "I don't know whether I can or not. I couldn't have the other afternoon. There was such a mob there it would have been impossible. You just don't know the situation down here."

After days of such fencing, Robert Kennedy thought he had the governor's assurance that the resistance would end. Barnett had already made himself a hero across the state. In terms of practical politics, he could now quit well ahead. Only the fanatics could expect or want him to carry on any further in a struggle that he and Mississippi were bound to lose.

Nick Katzenbach flew to Memphis to lead a motor caravan of two dozen federal marshals to Oxford. They were allowed to carry sidearms but told to keep them unloaded. Since the orders did not make clear what they should do with their bullets, the marshals kept them in their hands and pockets. The cars were within twenty miles of the campus when a communications plane, circling above them, relayed an order from the Attorney General to turn back. Night was falling, and two hundred state policemen with steel helmets, gas masks, and clubs were deployed around the university grounds.

Another force of deputies and sheriffs waited at a railroad bridge that divided the campus from the town. Even more threatening was the presence of hundreds of unin-

vited rednecks who had swarmed in from the backlands,
eager to join in a fight. Darkness is the best time for mob
action. Wisely, Bobby Kennedy decided to call off the attempt.

Meredith was riding in a car with McShane and Doar.
They turned off the main highway and drove five miles to
Batesville, the nearest town, to call the Attorney General
from a pay phone. They confirmed the order and rejoined
the caravan.

Barnett had used the police powers of his state, not to
preserve order, as he later maintained, but to escalate his
battle with the central government. We were now on the
edge of the gravest conflict between federal and state authority since the Civil War.

A little after noon on Sunday, September 30, 1962,
Bobby Kennedy notified Barnett that the President had ordered fifteen hundred U. S. Army troops to stand by in
Memphis, and had put the Mississippi National Guard
into federal service, for use if needed. Meredith would be
brought to the campus and enrolled in the university
shortly after dark, preceded by a convoy of marshals. A majority of the students would not return to the campus until
Monday morning The arrangements were reviewed with
the head of the state police.

The move seemed to be working. Meredith was escorted
through the police lines, registered, and quietly installed in
a dormitory room.

But soon a crowd began to gather, surrounding the U.S.
marshals who had taken up positions outside the Lyceum
Building. At first they seemed to be mostly students. Then

the word spread, the agitators came running, and the mood turned ugly and threatening. Many were armed with clubs and shotguns. They came in cars and trucks that bore license plates from all over the South and as far away as California.

Meredith had been assigned to Baxter Hall, a nearly empty dormitory at the far end of the campus. When the trouble started, he could see or hear little of it. He read a newspaper and, exhausted and relieved, fell asleep around ten o'clock. He may have been one of the few people on the Ole Miss campus to sleep through the night.

About the time James Meredith was reading his newspaper, President Kennedy went on national television to report on the situation at Oxford. Why did he decide to go public? I believe he did so partly to dispel the rumors, already in print, of a "deal" between the government and Barnett. The most popular version had Barnett permitting Meredith to enroll, after which the marshals would withdraw. Meredith felt, not unreasonably, that he would be doomed the moment he was left unguarded.

The President decided it was time to let Mississippi, and the country, know that the U.S. government was not going halfway. He appealed to the students and citizens of the state to uphold the law. Kennedy did not mince words. Had the state used its police powers to support the orders of the court, and not to block them; had the university fulfilled its role, a peaceable solution would have been possible without federal intervention.

Twice during the night, as the mob raged out of control, the Mississippi police moved—or were ordered—off the

campus, leaving the marshals alone and exposed. For some
six hours the marshals had held their ground although
pelted with rocks, bottles, scrap iron, and, finally, Molotov
cocktails. In the jaws of a rioting mob, their conduct was
brave and prudent. Their orders were to disperse the crowd
but not to provoke it. When they began to be pushed
back, the marshals fired tear gas.

Before the night was over, random sniper shots had
killed one onlooker and a French reporter. At midnight the
President ordered in the U.S. troops. The guard unit he
had activated that morning was part of the 155th Infantry,
one of the ten oldest regiments in the Union, whose soldiers had been decorated in six wars dating back to 1865.

Afterward, one account of what had happened reached a
chilling conclusion:*

> Between noon and midnight on September 30, 1962,
> this nation came within one man's nod of a state-sized
> civil war. The riot that exploded at the University of Mis-
> sissippi in Oxford brought death to two men and injuries
> to hundreds. But it was a pep rally compared to what al-
> most happened.
>
> A group of Mississippi leaders had been secretly plan-
> ning to form a wall of unarmed bodies that would not
> yield until knocked down and trod upon by Federals.
> Many segregationists were prepared to go to jail. Many
> were ready to fight with fists, rocks and clubs. Some re-
> solved to stand until shot down. Others planned to defy
> the orders of their leaders and conceal pistols on their per-
> sons.

The man who could have nodded, of course, was Gover-

* George B. Leonard, T. George Harris, and Christopher S. Wren, "How
a Secret Deal Prevented a Massacre at Ole Miss," *Look* magazine (Dec.
31, 1962), p. 19.

nor Barnett. To his credit, or because of blind luck, he did not nod. Tension ebbed away. The university, and the racists who had sought to make the incident into a spark that would ignite their cause, accepted the integration the court had ordered. The focus of the civil rights dispute shifted to other places.

It would have been easy, at that point, to close the books and forget what had happened—easy, but hardly realistic. Governor Barnett had defied the authority of the United States, and the Fifth Circuit was determined that the issue would not be allowed to drift and be forgotten. It perceived that the issue of Meredith's admission was not simply whether the University of Mississippi should be integrated. It was also whether the national government indeed governed.

The charges filed by the Department of Justice specified that the conduct of Governor Barnett had been in willful disregard and in defiance of the restraining orders issued by the court, and that by his acts he encouraged law enforcement officials and others in Mississippi to obstruct and prevent the entry of Meredith onto the campus of the university.

At the pretrial hearing before the Fifth Circuit Court, Barnett's lawyers raised the question of whether he was entitled to a jury trial. The court, sitting *en banc*, with eight judges present (and the ninth excused for poor health), considered the motion at length. When the time came to decide, the court divided four and four and certified the question to the U. S. Supreme Court.

Months later, on the morning the case was to be heard

by the high court, I appeared at the Justice Department in a business suit. Archibald Cox, then the solicitor general, later to be the first Watergate prosecutor, did a double-take. "Leon," he said, "you can't go into court like that. You're representing the government. You have to wear a morning coat and tails."

"Don't have any," I said. Formal attire, although de rigueur for government attorneys in cases before the high court, was not a tradition that appealed to me. But Cox insisted, and borrowed a cutaway from a member of his staff who, regrettably, weighed forty pounds less than I did. I felt like a penguin stuffed into that morning suit. All during the argument, I was worried that the seams would split each time I sat down.

Both the borrowed clothes and our position held up. The Supreme Court ruled, five to four, that a defendant in a criminal contempt proceeding was *not* entitled to a jury trial, so long as the punishment did not exceed that for a petty criminal offense. This was interpreted to mean not more than six months in jail.

After the Supreme Court ruling, there was another pre-trial conference before the Fifth Circuit. Briefs were submitted on such questions as where the trial should be held and whether the court should sit *en banc*. The points were soon to be academic.

Two and a half years had now passed since the ordeal at the University of Mississippi. Barnett's term as governor had ended. He had vowed to the people of Mississippi that he would go to jail to preserve segregation. He had not and would not. A majority of the justices believed that the changed conditions had brought about full compliance with the court's orders, that Barnett had, in effect, purged himself, and the suit could be dismissed.

And so it was done. Although the dismissal was widely publicized I did not receive so much as a single letter of complaint, or approval. Nick Katzenbach, who by then had succeeded Bobby Kennedy as Attorney General, told me no one had written him, either. The howls that deafened me when I was preparing to prosecute Barnett had no echo when the calm operation of our system of justice let him off.

I have often wondered, over the years, what impact Governor Barnett's defiance of the orders of the Fifth Circuit would have had on the administration of justice, had the court not immediately directed that criminal contempt proceedings be brought. Others very likely would have been encouraged to follow his foolhardy example. The rule of law would have been weakened, and the struggle for equal rights made more difficult, and bloodier.

Unquestionably, any citizen has the right to disagree with a court's decision and to offer constructive criticism. Indeed, it is the obligation of informed citizens to do so. But we must not confuse those who honestly differ with those who seize upon an unpopular decision and exploit it for unworthy purposes. For those who find a decision of the courts unwise or unjust, there are orderly ways to seek redress—through appeals to higher courts, through legislation and constitutional amendment. Blind emotion too often prevents the dissenter from realizing the importance of preserving the system itself, regardless of what current issues may strain it.

The South, in particular, went through a moral convulsion after the Supreme Court's ruling on desegregation in 1954. So much has been said and written about the roots, the traditions, the sense of identity, and the tragic dimensions of this region, we sometimes overlook a central truth: that progress became possible when a number of southern judges stood up for what was right, and suffered the abuse and contempt of their neighbors.

The painful odyssey continues. John Kennedy was murdered one month after the Barnett case went before the Supreme Court. Robert Kennedy was killed in 1968.

Ross Barnett is long gone from the political stage, his views, like those of his state, mellowed by time. At eighty he still practices law, and in 1978 defended a Mississippian in a murder trial in Texas. Barnett and his wife live in a two-story, red brick home in a quiet Jackson neighborhood. He teaches a Sunday school class and drives to Oxford to cheer for the Ole Miss football team, whose star players are now black as well as white.

James Meredith earned a degree in political science at Ole Miss. Meredith, too, lives in Jackson, and owns several businesses, including a bar once frequented by members of the Ku Klux Klan. He has run for state office, and lost, as a Democrat and a Republican. His children attend private school.

I believe the country has learned from the past. We know now that, sadly, so many who strike at our system of justice are often the loudest at proclaiming their patriotism. They act in the name of that which they would eventually destroy.

8

The Inquest

At times we see life as a sort of six-day bicycle race. Heads down, we pedal furiously, quite without concern for the rest of the field, intent on going nowhere quickly.

Then a tragedy of unthinkable dimension occurs—as on November 22, 1963—and we are reminded of what is real in the world, and we know our lives will never seem quite the same again.

Only a few months before, I had finished my work on the Ross Barnett case. My decision to assist the Justice Department, greeted by so much disfavor in my home city, had not hurt me or my firm, after all. Some of the same clients who had threatened to take away their business were now begging us to represent them. One man even got down on the floor.

I had been absorbed that morning in the legal papers resting on my lap, which were the reason for my flight to Dallas—a suit involving a client. I was not even aware that we were circling Love Field until the squawk of the captain's voice filled the cabin: "Sorry about the delay. Seems the tower is waiting for Air Force One to touch down. We're in a holding pattern, along with all the other traffic. Should be on the ground in just a few minutes."

Then it dawned on me that President Kennedy was to speak in Dallas that afternoon. I had been in Washington for a few days and had lost track of the news at home. The President had spent the night in Fort Worth, after receiving a hero's welcome earlier in the day in Houston, where two previous visits had proven historic for him. He had confronted the Baptist ministers there in the campaign of 1960, and a year later, at Rice Stadium, he had declared America's intention to put a man on the moon "in this decade." He won his audience on the second occasion by addressing man's need to challenge his spirit: "Why sail the ocean? Why climb the highest mountain? Why does Rice play Texas?"

Looking ahead to the 1964 election, Jack Kennedy wanted to carry Texas and he wanted to carry it big. He needed an undivided Democratic party. He had decided to make a swing across the state in an attempt to narrow the space between the rival factions headed by Governor John Connally, on the right, and Senator Ralph Yarborough, on the left. His Vice-President, Lyndon Johnson, was with him in the role of deputy peacemaker.

That effort, I thought, would make for some lively reading, and dinner party talk, for the next several days. Then I put the subject out of my mind. As I stepped into a taxi, a little after eleven o'clock, the day was crisp and clear, the sun high and butter-colored. A nice day for a motorcade.

My meeting, with other lawyers involved in the case, was at a men's club in downtown Dallas: the kind of traditional club where the rooms are private, the wood dark, the furniture old, and where the waiters enter and leave without being noticed. At about twelve-thirty we decided to break for lunch. We were still reading our menus when a waiter appeared at the door and shouted, "They've been shot! President Kennedy and Mr. Johnson. Somebody shot them in their car."

I felt myself freeze. I knew Kennedy, admired and believed in him. Lyndon Johnson was a client and a friend. A television set was nearby and someone rushed over and clicked it on. We all moved or adjusted our chairs to face the screen. Others had quietly drifted into the room. Any thought of work had vanished. No attempt was made at conversation. We were as one, limp and lifeless, talking in fragments.

It soon became apparent that the waiter's information was only half right. From the TV reports we learned that Connally, not Johnson, had been wounded. Kennedy's condition was uncertain. We watched and listened until all hope was gone. The meeting broke up in a sad and mumbled confusion, even as Lyndon Johnson was flying back to Washington on Air Force One, whose arrival a few brief hours before had delayed my own.

Unspoken in that room was one thought. A Texan, Lyndon Johnson, was now the President. The power was shifting from Boston to Austin. But there was no joy in any of us, no heart to think beyond the moment. The tragedy of

John Kennedy's death, for the nation, would be a long
while measured.

I flew back to Houston. By the following Thursday,
Thanksgiving Day, I had driven to my ranch near Austin. I
still felt subdued and unsettled from the events in Dallas.
There I received a phone call from Waggoner Carr, the attorney general of Texas. Waggoner said it was important,
urgent, that he see me. I invited him to the ranch.

I knew, in a vague way, that the call would be related to
the assassination. Within hours after the Kennedy funeral,
Carr had sought and received President Johnson's approval
to form a court of inquiry in Texas to investigate the
killing. Carr had gone on television to announce that fact
to the nation.

Carr is a slender, urbane fellow, nice-looking, with wavy
gray hair. His manner is brisk, but not abrasive. He was
then at the height of his political ambitions. But he also
felt a loyalty to the state of Texas, which had then a desperate need to absolve itself of guilt. The President, people
kept saying, could have been killed anywhere—but it happened in Texas. Though his alleged assassin was a Marxist,
threats to the President's safety—written and rumored—
had come from the extremists of the right wing.

Carr and I spent that entire afternoon talking: about the
horror of Kennedy's death; the arrest of Lee Harvey Oswald and his murder, in the basement of the Dallas jail, by
Jack Ruby; about the temper loose in the land, and the
need for swift action in pursuit of the facts. He asked me
to serve as his special counsel on the court of inquiry, and I

accepted. It never occurred to me that I should do otherwise.

At that point, the Warren Commission did not exist, and it would come into being a few days later over the personal reluctance of the man whose name it would bear. In that first disconnected week after the President fell, who really knew what was needed or possible or suitable? Oswald was in his grave, and one cannot prosecute a dead man. Jack Ruby was in jail, and any hearings had to be held in a way that would not prejudice his trial.

Now, some fifteen years later, it seems naïve even to suggest that the public could have accepted as credible the investigation of John Kennedy's death by a panel in the state where he died. But for the moment at least, ours was the only legal authority proposed. Having observed the unrelenting attacks aimed at the Warren Commission, I can only guess at the mockery if the Texas plan had prevailed.

That thought occurred to someone in the White House, too. Within hours after my name was connected to the Texas investigation, I received a phone call from Nick Katzenbach, then the deputy attorney general, and Abe Fortas, long a Johnson adviser and soon to be a Supreme Court justice. They asked if I would fly to Washington as soon as possible.

Once I arrived, it did not take long to learn how serious a problem had developed. The city was seething with rumors and accusations surrounding John Kennedy's death. Some sources in Europe had jumped on the story that Johnson himself had disposed of Kennedy in order to ascend to the presidency. Any investigation that was localized in Texas would be, to put it gently, under suspicion.

Meanwhile, Johnson had sent two emissaries to Earl
Warren to ask if he would head a national commission
created to establish the truth and end, if possible, the bi-
zarre stories and speculation. Warren had declined.

But the new President invited the Chief Justice to the
White House and put his gift of persuasion to work. He
did not need to tell him about the urgency of putting the
rumors to rest, or to remind him that the country was torn
and grieving and hungry for answers. Warren had taken
Kennedy's death in a personal way. "It was like losing one
of my own sons," he said. "You know, he was just a little
older than my oldest boy."

Warren had delivered the eulogy on a Sunday afternoon
in the rotunda of the Capitol, as he stood beside the flag-
draped casket. From the depths of him, he spoke of "the
hatred that consumes people, the false accusations that di-
vide us, and the bitterness that begets violence."

He knew about the hate and the accusations. He had
been a target of the John Birch Society. He was no longer
young and his own responsibilities were towering. It was
not difficult to see why he would be reluctant to take on
this new and emotionally charged assignment.

But Lyndon Johnson kept talking. He mentioned the
special trust that foreign lands would have in an inquiry
headed by Earl Warren. And he *knew*, he said, that if
America was under attack by foreign forces and needed
him, Earl Warren would get back into his soldier's suit
from World War I.

Warren accepted the chairmanship of the President's

Commission on the Assassination of President Kennedy. As he left the Oval Office, there were tears in his eyes.

The group he headed quickly came to be known as the Warren Commission. Warren always referred to it, faithfully, as the Kennedy Commission. The membership was composed of two senators, Richard B. Russell and John Sherman Cooper; two representatives, Hale Boggs and Gerald Ford; and two distinguished lawyers who had served both Republican and Democratic Presidents, Allen Dulles and John J. McCloy. At Warren's suggestion, the commission chose J. Lee Rankin, a former solicitor general, as its chief counsel.

Now remained the question, the slightly sensitive political question, of what to do about the Texas court of inquiry. The new President himself had approved it, and he could not very well leave Waggoner Carr hanging out to dry. In short order, I concluded the only solution was to merge the two bodies. From the standpoint of Lyndon Johnson it was essential, and he gave me the task of convincing Warren, who was opposed to any Texas connection.

I met privately with the Chief Justice, and argued that the attorney general of Texas did have an interest in this matter. Warren, who could say no with a touch of flattery, told me, "Leon, I would like to have had you head our staff. But your connection with the Texas group makes that impossible."

Another meeting was arranged that included Carr, as well as Katzenbach and Archibald Cox from the Justice Department. Warren kept his back to Carr most of the meeting and never spoke to him directly. I managed to deflect a few of the Chief Justice's questions his way by saying, "I think Waggoner can answer that better than I."

Although his attitude toward Carr was, at best, tepid, Warren was not a rude man. I sensed no personal dislike, but rather a feeling on his part—a hope, actually—that he could keep politics out of the hearings. A noble goal, and one he tried mightily to enforce. Of course, politics is not incompatible with the truth. It just takes longer. The FBI, the Secret Service, the Dallas police, all had been embarrassed by the failure to protect Kennedy. And the state of Texas, from the beginning, felt itself on trial.

As a lawyer with no political record, I was acceptable to Warren. But we did not want a token Texan, and the Chief Justice did not want a Texas annex. Finally he agreed to a compromise that would make it unnecessary to put in motion the court of inquiry. Carr and I and his other special counsel—Robert G. Storey, dean of the SMU law school and a former president of the ABA—were to work directly with the commission. One or more of us would be present at the hearings of the commission. We would interview witnesses living in Texas, obtain the co-operation of state officials, and submit investigative reports. We reserved the right to publish a supplemental report to the findings of the Warren Commission.

After the details were worked out, Carr and I stopped off at the White House to see President Johnson. It was nearly 10 P.M., but he was in the swimming pool, paddling around with one of his aides, Jack Valenti. Johnson was wearing swim trunks, a social convention he did not always observe.

The conversation was light and good-natured. It was the night the President asked me what I wanted, what job, and I told him there was nothing. When we left, Carr grinned and said, "You're stuck. He's going to bring you up here, sure as hell."

"No, he isn't," I said, "because I won't let him." I had found that I enjoyed Washington best a few days at a time. When I finally did stay longer—two weeks short of a year—the President who brought me to town was Richard Nixon.

Lyndon Johnson was under no illusion about the difficulty of the task that faced the Warren Commission. He had an instinct for the popular mind. "Ten per cent will think Oswald was framed," he said. "Ten per cent won't believe he was acting alone. Ten per cent will claim he was working for the FBI or the CIA or both. And another 10 per cent will say the whole thing is a hoax and Kennedy is still alive. You start out with 40 per cent of the people who won't want to be convinced, whatever the truth is."

I was not so skeptical. As the evidence accumulated, as the kooks and cranks were screened and dismissed, and the motives of some of the so-called conspiracy buffs became clear, I grew more and more confident that the major answers were already known.

On September 24, 1964, Earl Warren submitted to the President a report which concluded that Lee Harvey Oswald assassinated President Kennedy and fired the shots that wounded Governor Connally, and killed Officer J. D. Tippitt. It also concluded that the acts of Lee Harvey Oswald were not caused by any conspiracy, domestic or foreign, to assassinate President Kennedy.

Not in my weakest moments did I imagine that fifteen years later the report would still be the target of bitter controversy, or that new assassination theories would be rolling off the presses like salted peanuts.

The impact of John Kennedy's death has been overshadowed now by the ghoulish industry that grew out of it. Over forty books have been published attacking the Warren Report, or introducing new theories. Some of these books have been described as "scholarly," which means they contain footnotes. Seniors at the UCLA Law School made a study in 1966 of the best known of the conspiracy books, *Rush to Judgment*, by Mark Lane. Their research found that 90 per cent of his footnotes did not check out. They concluded that Lane "twists evidence out of context and often uses himself as his own expert witness."*

So we have had the theory of the two Oswalds, the two John Kennedys, the second gun, Oswald as "the Manchurian Candidate," and conspiracies promoted by the Soviets, by Castro, by the Mafia, the FBI, the CIA, the oil cartel. Nothing is easier to create than an atmosphere of suspicion. Nothing is more difficult to dispel, so long as the crackpots and the gullible abound.

Critics of the Warren Report pick and choose among conflicting memories and minor inconsistencies. They play

* R. W. Lewis, "The Scavengers," *World Journal Tribune Sunday Magazine* (Jan. 22, 1967).

up the testimony of untrained and unreliable witnesses, while ignoring or glossing over the hard physical evidence of Oswald's guilt. He bought the rifle found at the Book Depository and left his palm print on it. Two bullet fragments from this rifle were retrieved from the front of the President's car, and another bullet from the hospital where he was pronounced dead. Eyewitnesses identified Oswald as the man who killed Officer Tippitt.

If Oswald was really innocent, then Robert Kennedy, the Attorney General, the head of the Justice Department, had to be covering up for the person who murdered his brother. I find that harder to believe than do some of the assassination fans.

As for Jack Ruby, his killing of Oswald was a quirk, an accident of time and chance. Beyond any possible doubt, Ruby could not have planned the shooting of the President's assassin. He stumbled into it.

Oswald was to be transferred from the city jail to the county jail at ten o'clock Sunday morning. At 10:19 A.M., Ruby, still in his bedclothes, received a phone call from a nineteen-year-old stripper named Karen Bennett Carlin, who worked under the name of Little Lynn at Ruby's night club, the Carousel. She needed twenty-five dollars to pay her rent and to buy groceries.

At 11:17 A.M., Ruby paid for the money order at the Western Union office a block from the Dallas city jail. The time was stamped on three documents, including his receipt. Oswald had been held upstairs for questioning, delaying by more than an hour his transfer to the county jail. At 11:21, he was led down to the basement, where

Jack Ruby lunged past the waiting reporters and television cameras and blew a hole in Oswald's stomach. Four minutes. Just enough time for Ruby to cross the street.

Can anyone really make a case for Jack Ruby's being a part of a conspiracy? A belief that Ruby was hired to silence Oswald must accommodate the odd notion that a man bent on murder would risk losing his only chance in order to wire a money order to a stripper.

On one point we can all agree. Ruby's shot made it impossible for the central mystery of John Kennedy's death ever to be solved to universal satisfaction.

Why did Oswald kill the President?

Had Oswald lived, he would have told us. At some point during his trial, he would have admitted—no, taken credit for—his ghastly deed. In such a way he would have responded to the spotlight, to the sense of power he surely would have felt from holding the attention of so many. Perhaps he would have thrown in a little martyr talk, how he did it for Cuba, for freedom, for oppressed people everywhere.

Of course, we have no such confession. What we are left with is the record of his life. Oswald was a chronic malcontent, a complainer, a factory reject, a failure at whatever he did and wherever he went. He was a school dropout. Quit the Marines. Fled from his own country. Defected to Russia, grew disenchanted there, made a half-hearted attempt to slash his wrists because the Soviets wouldn't accept him as the hero he wanted to be. He returned to America. Thought about going back to Russia. Thought about Cuba. And finally, in his own warped way, decided that his best chance to become famous was to kill someone who already was.

In her testimony before the Warren Commission, his wife, Marina, told us much about the nature of Lee Harvey Oswald:

"He liked some things in Russia, liked some things here, didn't like some things there, and didn't like some things here. And I am convinced that as much as he knew about Cuba, all he knew was from books and so on . . . he would not have liked it there, either. Only on the moon, perhaps."

Still, the theories keep coming. Some see in Oswald's attempt to reach Cuba, his visit to the Cuban embassy in Mexico, the movements of a spy. If Lee Harvey Oswald was a Soviet agent, then Marina Oswald is the lost daughter of the Czar, Anastasia. Oswald was a public nuisance, who handed out pamphlets on the street and carried a picket to protest American policies. He fought, rather badly, and got himself arrested. If the KGB selects its spies from such material, then the wrong Marx—Groucho, not Karl—founded communism.

If I state these opinions strongly now, it is because I regret that those of us who believed in the Warren Report, and in the evidence, failed to raise our voices more aggressively fifteen years ago. I thought the critics were so obvious in their distortions, so wildly off the mark in their conclusions, that the best course was to ignore them. I was wrong. As for the books that abuse the report, the most remarkable thing about them is the seriousness with which they have been taken.

In all these years no hard evidence has been produced to contradict the findings of the Warren Commission. No conspirator. No second gun or fourth bullet. No documents that even hint at Oswald's having worked for the FBI or the CIA. Ironically, most of the speculation has been based on how the critics read the Warren Report, how they interpreted the testimony.

Any picture of Lee Harvey Oswald as a spy, a dupe, a victim, must collide at once with that drawn by his widow, the mother of his children, who had above anyone else a need to believe he was not an assassin.

As a trial lawyer, I found Marina Oswald a convincing and natural witness: a little nervous, a little awed, not glib or facile. She was the first of 550 witnesses to appear before the Warren Commission, on the morning of February 3, 1964. She had gained a better command of English since the tragedy in Dallas, but her words were not picked with the kind of care that makes you suspect you are hearing a performance.

I listened intently as she told how Oswald had shot at and missed General Edwin Walker, a stalwart of the far right. Walker was a political opposite of John Kennedy. It suggested to me that Oswald was simply interested in killing someone, anyone, of public visibility.

"Before the incident with General Walker," she said, "I know that Lee was preparing for something. He took photographs of that house and he told me not to enter his room. . . . Later, after he had fired, he told me about it.

"That evening he went out . . . it got to be about 10 or 10:30, he wasn't home yet, and I began to be worried. Perhaps even later. Then I went to his room. Somehow, I was drawn into it—you know—I was pacing around. Then I saw a note there . . . it said, 'If I am arrested' and there are certain other questions, such as, for example, the key to the mailbox is in such and such a place, and that he left me some money to last me for some time, and I couldn't understand at all what can he be arrested for. When he came back I asked him what had happened. He was very pale . . . and he told me not to ask him any questions. He only told me that he had shot at General Walker. I didn't sleep all night. I thought that at any minute now, the police would come. Of course, I wanted to ask him a great deal. But in his state I decided I had best leave him alone—it would be purposeless to question him."

The next morning, Marina said, she and Lee argued about his attempt to kill General Walker. "I told him that he had no right to kill people in peacetime, he had no right to take their life because not everybody has the same ideas as he has. People cannot be all alike. He said that this was a very bad man, that he was a fascist, that he was the leader of a fascist organization . . . he said if someone had killed Hitler in time it would have saved many lives. I told him that this is no method to prove your ideas, by means of a rifle."

Oswald learned in that morning's newspaper that he had missed his target. When he fired, he told his wife, he did not know whether he had hit Walker or not. "He ran several kilometers and then took the bus. And he turned on the radio and listened, but there were no reports." In the newspaper, Walker was quoted as saying he had moved his head and the bullet just missed him. Oswald, according to Marina, was irritated. "He said only that he had taken very good aim, that it was just chance that caused him to miss. He was very sorry that he had not hit him."

When she was asked whether her husband had owned a rifle or a shotgun at the time he lived in the Soviet Union, she said, "I don't know the difference. One and the other shoots. You men. That is your business."

The Chief Justice, who happens to be fond of hunting, broke in to remark, "My wife wouldn't know the difference, so it is all right."

There was clearly sympathy in the room for Marina Oswald. She was a vulnerable figure, left alone and nearly friendless, the widow of a man who would be remembered by most Americans as a kind of monster. She described a man who was erratic and tense and sometimes pathetic. He dreamed of great achievements, and once boasted he would be a prime minister in twenty years, though he did not say of what country. On occasion he beat her. Marina said it was not always Lee's fault. Once, depressed, she wrote a letter to an old boyfriend in Russia. The letter was returned for the lack of a penny's postage. Oswald read it and blacked her eye.

But often the questions came back to the gun, the 6.5 mm Mannlicher-Carcano that fired the bullets that killed John Kennedy.

Marina was living in the home of a Russian-speaking friend, a Mrs. Ruth Paine, on the day of the assassination. She was watching television when Mrs. Paine told her the President had been shot. "We both turned pale," she said.

"I went to my room and cried." A few minutes later, Mrs. Paine walked in and said, "By the way, they fired from the building in which Lee is working." Immediately she ran to the garage, where Oswald kept his rifle in a rolled-up blanket on the floor. The blanket was still there. She thought she saw the outline of a gun.

When the police knocked on the door of her home, Mrs. Paine startled them by saying, "I've been expecting you all." Asked why, she replied, "Just as soon as I heard where the shooting happened, I knew there would be someone out."

Mrs. Paine translated for Marina when the officers questioned her. When one asked if her husband owned a rifle, she said, "No," and a minute later corrected herself. "Yes, he does have." She led them to the garage and pointed to the blanket. "Well, now they will find it," she thought. But the blanket was empty. "Then, of course," Marina testified, "I already knew it was Lee."

The day after his arrest, Marina was allowed to see her husband. She did not accuse him of killing the President, or even ask—"after all, he was my husband." But she knew. "He said that I should not worry, that everything would turn out well. But I could see by his eyes that he was guilty. Rather, he tried to appear to be brave. However, by his eyes I could tell that he was afraid. He said good-by to me with his eyes."

After the police had left, she found her husband's wedding ring in their bedroom. He had not expected to live through the day. In tracing his movements after the assassination, I was struck by that very thought. He had not

planned an escape. There were no conspirators to help
him, real or imagined. It was simply a matter of one
wretched individual, a loner, surprised at finding himself
still alive, wondering where to turn. He began to think he
might get away with it. He clung to that idea after his cap-
ture, when he loudly professed his innocence. When Marina saw him, he was still swinging between fear and bra-
vado.

Asked in front of the Warren Commission what she
thought her husband's motive was, Marina answered:
"From everything that I know . . . and of the events that
transpired, I can conclude that he wanted in any way,
whether good or bad, to do something that would make
him outstanding, that he would be known in history."

If the commission perceived Oswald's wife as truthful
and convincing, its critics relied on the testimony of his
mother, in some ways the most fascinating character of all.
Anyone who wishes to believe that Oswald was framed, or
was the unwitting foil of an FBI conspiracy, or had a double, should understand that these and several other
theories were first given circulation by the mother. "As we
all know," she said, offering as fact one of the more gro-
tesque rumors, "President Kennedy was a dying man. So I
say it is possible that my son was chosen to shoot him in a
mercy killing for the security of the country."

She came before the commission clutching a large black
handbag crammed with letters, newspaper clippings, and
magazine articles—her "documents," she called them. She
kept fishing through her portable file cabinet without ever
seeming to find just the right piece of paper. Marguerite

Oswald was an odd and perplexing witness, who made repeated references to her son's innocence and yet could wax indignant because President Johnson "owed" her a private interview as "the mother of Lee Harvey Oswald," as though Johnson had ascended to that office through her son's graces.

She alternately boasted of her refusal to give a statement to the FBI or the CIA, then complained because her son and daughter-in-law had been interviewed. She swore the FBI in Dallas had taken her testimony for only ten minutes. When she was showed a twenty-eight-page transcript, equal to roughly two hours of questioning, and the tape itself was played back, she insisted it must have been faked.

To illustrate her struggle to overcome adversity, she told a remarkable story of taking her three young sons with her as she broke into the apartment of a woman who was entertaining her second husband.

Mrs. Oswald was quick to show her emotions, but never so openly as when she discussed money. She debated for several minutes whether or not to turn over to the commission a collection of Lee's boyhood pictures, three of which she had sold to news magazines for fifty dollars apiece. She decided to keep them. She expressed her concern, and her puzzlement, that Marina had received donations of around $35,000 from the American public, and Mrs. Tippitt, the widow of the policeman, several times as much. "My contributions up to now," she complained, "are just a little over $900. That is the money that has been given direct to me, the mother of Lee Harvey Oswald."

For nearly fifteen pages of testimony, Lee Rankin attempted to draw out of Mrs. Oswald her reasons for believing her son was an agent of the U.S. government. He began one sentence with, "Can't we get down to—"

"No, sir, we cannot," she interrupted. "I am sorry. This is my life. I cannot survive in this world unless I know I have my American way of life and can start from the very beginning. . . . I am the accused mother of this man. . . . And I am going to do everything I can to try and prove he is innocent."

It developed that she based her theory on a trip she made to Washington when she was trying to arrange her son's return from Russia, and when an official at the State Department treated her with courtesy.

"Now, one other thing," she went on. "When Marina and Lee returned from Russia, and they were at my daughter-in-law's home, Robert's home, and I came in from my job in the country to see them, I said—up until this time, gentlemen, I thought Russians were peasant-looking people, like the public. And I said, 'Lee, she doesn't look Russian at all. She looks American.' He said, 'Of course, Mother, that is why I married her, is because she looks American.' In front of my daughter-in-law and Robert. He bragged that she looked like an American girl."

RANKIN: How does that show he was an agent at that time? I don't understand that.

MRS. OSWALD: I don't either. But I am telling you the expressions. He is making a point. Lee loved his work, and Lee loved the Marines. . . .

I was spellbound. The members of the commission

looked at each other, quizzically, as she talked. Mrs. Oswald
had retained Mark Lane as her attorney, and his fine hand
could be seen in some of her testimony, and particularly in
her request that Lane be allowed to sit in on the hearings.
Actually, she identified him as her late son's attorney. I am
not sure who fell into whose hands, but let us say that
Mark Lane and Mrs. Oswald found each other, and justice
was served. Since Mrs. Oswald was already represented by
counsel, John F. Doyle, the commission turned down
Lane's offer to take part in the hearings.

Mrs. Oswald gave the impression of one who has had to
fight every day for her basic human rights. For security
reasons, the family had been moved to a hotel outside of
Dallas after the assassination. She resented it when the Secret Service made up separate sleeping rooms for herself
and for Marina and her baby. She saw it as an attempt to
keep them apart. "I have a very dignified way about me,"
she testified. "I didn't say a word. What I did—I sat up in
a chair all night long in the living room . . . rather than be
pushed aside."

She spoke often of how good she was to her daughter-in-
law and how much she loved her. But once, when she
dropped by her house and found her gone, she suspected
Marina of seeing another man. She parked her car and
waited in a Montgomery Ward parking lot most of the afternoon. That night Lee gave Marina another black eye.
She had gone off with her two little girls to visit friends
and take an English lesson.

Of her mother-in-law, Marina had said, "It seemed peculiar to me and [I] didn't want to believe it, but [Lee] did

not love his mother. She was not quite a normal woman. . . .

"I was always sorry for her because Lee did not want to live with her. I understood her motherly concern. But in view of the fact of everything that happened later, her appearances in the radio, in the press, I do not think that she is a very sound thinking woman, and I think that part of the guilt is hers . . . if her relationship with me was good, it was not sincere. I think that she does not like me. I don't think that she simply is able to like me. There were some violent scenes. She didn't want to listen to anyone. There were hysterics. Everyone was guilty of everything and no one understood her."

Every lawyer has had an experience with the Captain Queeg kind of witness, the ones who can't stop clicking the ball bearings, whose voice and mannerisms reveal their own paranoia. There was nothing subtle about Mrs. Oswald. With her own words, she made it clear that she had three objectives: to defend herself, to defend her son, and to make some money—in which order one cannot be sure.

Others are in the conspiracy game for financial gain, notoriety, excitement, or all of these. There are some who are well intentioned and sincere. They simply cannot accept Oswald's guilt, because to do so is to accept a murder without meaning.

We have now seen the disclosure of 80,000 pages of FBI documents relating to the Kennedy assassination. We have seen a stumbling and comic attempt by a congressional subcommittee to reopen the investigation. Yet nothing has been brought forward by anyone to shake the verdict of the

Warren Commission that Lee Harvey Oswald, alone, killed John Kennedy.†

In no period of history, in no other country, has a government conducted so thorough and scrupulous an investigation. Along with the testimony of its own witnesses, the Warren Commission drew on the material contained in 25,000 FBI interviews and 1,500 more by the CIA. In Texas, we filed our supplemental report, accepting the findings of the commission. Bob Storey added a passage about the rule of law, and Waggoner Carr inserted a sentence defending the Dallas police, and our work was done.

When Earl Warren submitted the final report, and the twenty-six volumes of hearings, he told the President, "This has been a long and depressing job."

For the record, Lyndon Johnson's first words were, "It's pretty heavy."

† On December 30, 1978, the major conclusion of the Warren Report —one gun, one gunman—was disputed by the House Assassinations Committee. Reversing its own findings in the final week of a two-year inquiry, the committee accepted the theories of a second gun and a fourth bullet, and decided that John F. Kennedy's death was the result of a "probable" conspiracy. This assertion was based on evidence introduced at the eleventh hour, relying on a new science and a fifteen-year-old tape recording of uncertain custody made from the open radio of a police motorcycle that might have been two miles from the scene of the murder in Dallas. My own conclusion is that the committee could not bring itself to report what was already known fifteen years ago: that sufficient positive evidence does not exist to prove, or disprove, that Kennedy died by a conspiracy. The panel yielded to what had been the obvious temptation: to produce something dramatic to justify an effort that cost the public nearly $6 million.

9
The Court

The presentation of an oral argument to the Supreme Court has never been a relaxed experience for me. Usually I begin to get charged up a day or two before, and by the time the argument is presented I am tense and nervous.

I practically went into training for the Nixon case. I took brisk walks, sometimes jogged, and, when I could, escaped on the weekends to my ranch near Austin to clear trees and saw wood.

An incident involving the ranch brought home to me how tricky the road through Watergate would be, the tangled roots that waited there. Months before I was drawn into the Watergate case, while I was still the president of the American Bar Association, I invited Chief Justice Warren Burger and his wife to spend several days as our guests, enjoying the rustic life of the Texas hill country. At the last minute, they begged off.

Within a week after I arrived in Washington, to accept

the job as special prosecutor, I attended a dinner party hosted by the ABA president, Chesterfield Smith. Warren Burger was one of the speakers. When he rose, he said, dryly, "I've noticed in the papers that Leon Jaworski is in town," a reference to the stories that had chronicled my every move. Then he looked straight at me and said, "Leon, aren't you glad I didn't accept your invitation to the ranch?" Meaning, of course, that the case I had just undertaken could conceivably reach the highest court in the land, and the visit could have raised serious questions for one or both of us.

That almost encounter had no meaning as I approached the bench on the morning of July 8, 1974. Chief Justice Burger and I looked at each other as strangers.

Presenting an argument to the Supreme Court has always stirred in me special emotions. I am awed by the environment, the room like a cathedral, the very presence of the members of the Court. In my later years, it was difficult for me to understand why I still felt this way, inasmuch as nearly all of the justices were known to me, and some were quite close friends. But those relationships help not at all when the marshal calls the Court to order. I have needed no reminder of the responsibility, the stature, and the power invested there. I especially needed no such reminder on that Monday morning when the clerk called into session the case of *The United States of America* v. *Richard Nixon*.

The narrow issue to be decided by the court was whether Nixon, under a claim of executive privilege, could withhold evidence in a criminal matter. On April 16, 1974, I had asked Judge Sirica to issue a subpoena for the tapes of sixty-four White House conversations, of which at least eighteen would be crucial in exposing the full story of the cover-up.

The President's lawyers then moved to quash the subpoena. Among the guarantees I had been promised as special prosecutor was the right to contest any assertion by the President of executive privilege. Now his lawyers argued that I had no standing to do so. Inevitably, the Supreme Court would have to decide if Nixon could be forced to release the tapes; or if he, alone among all our citizens, was outside the judicial system.

His lawyer, James St. Clair, was in court arguing, in effect, that the President should not be in court. Our right to sue Richard Nixon had been challenged. My staff and I had spent endless, often tedious hours preparing for that attack.

The justices do not sit on ceremony. They tear into the arguments. They may wish to bring out the strength of your point. Sometimes they do so solely for the purpose of forcing you to proceed to the heart of your case, even though you may be trying to lay the groundwork for another issue. There are nine justices—on that day, eight—all free to ask any questions, whenever they wish. As I faced them, from my left, they were: Justices Lewis F. Powell, Jr., Thurgood Marshall, Potter Stewart, William O. Douglas, Chief Justice Warren E. Burger, William J. Brennan, Jr., Byron R. White, Harry A. Blackmun. The chair of William Rehnquist was empty. He had disqualified himself, having served on the legal staff of the Department of Justice.

While one is arguing a case, it is impossible to tell by the questions if a justice is friendly to one's cause. I could tell, for instance, that Justice Byron White hoped I would avoid any reference to the President's possible criminality, in view of his having been named by the grand jury as an unindicted co-conspirator. White wanted to move on to the matter of executive privilege, without my coupling it with the more sensitive question of the President's exposure.

But Potter Stewart, who had seemed to come down hard on me earlier, leaned on his elbows and said, encouragingly, "That's another string to your bow, isn't it?"

I was to be interrupted by the justices a total of 115 times in an hour. This was a time for fast answers, not sweeping oratory. Arguing before the high court is more like taking an oral quiz than trying a case. It was the same for Jim St. Clair, who questioned my claim that my mandate as special prosecutor allowed me to go to court to pursue evidence. I had quoted the words of Robert Bork, the acting Attorney General in the aftermath of the "Saturday Night Massacre." Bork had testified before Congress: ". . . Mr. Jaworski can go to court and test out any refusal to produce documents on the grounds of confidentiality."

Such issues are far removed from the crisp, mystery-story questions the public had buzzed about for months: Who authorized the Watergate break-in? And why? Who erased the eighteen-and-a-half-minute gap? Who was "Deep Throat"? By contrast, arguments over jurisdiction, procedures, and executive privilege are the stuff of law books, dry enough to put people to sleep.

Yet one of the things that the next generation will learn from Watergate is that the President is subject to the laws he has sworn to administer. His powers are not absolute.

All of our efforts in the Watergate investigation, including those of Archibald Cox and his staff before me, would have blown up in our faces if our arguments failed before the Supreme Court. I felt this pressure keenly. I had what lawyers call the laboring oar, the initial argument, which meant that I had to convince the Court of my authority to bring the President into court. Each side was granted ninety minutes for arguments, more time than I had ever heard of the Supreme Court allowing. I argued the first hour, my brilliant young counsel, Philip Lacovara, the closing half hour.

The questions came so fast that a notebook I had prepared, containing my handwritten notes, transcripts, and sources, was never opened. Some were piercing, in one or two instances disquieting, but no more for me than for Jim St. Clair. At one point, Justice Marshall sought to establish the limits of executive privilege, as defined by the President. He asked what would be the result if the evidence withheld by the President showed that he had accepted a bribe to appoint a person to the bench.

St. Clair: If the President did appoint such an individual . . . the remedy is he would be impeached . . .

Marshall: How are you going to impeach him if you don't know about it?

St. Clair: Well, if you know about it, then you can state the case. If you don't know about it, you don't have it.

Marshall: So there you are. You're on the prongs of a dilemma, huh?

St. Clair: No, I don't think so.

Marshall: If you know the President is doing something wrong, you can impeach him. But the only way you can find out is this way: you can't impeach him, so you don't impeach him. You lose me someplace along there.

St. Clair had made an eloquent statement of the President's first line of defense, arguing that "few [cases] in the nation's history have cut so close to the heart of the basic constitutional system in which our liberties are rooted. . . . The stakes are enormously high, from a constitutional standpoint. . . . At its core, this is a case that turns on the separation of powers."

I agreed with my brother's assessment, but we differed in our reading of how the separation of powers applied in this case. I attempted to turn around St. Clair's point:

"Now, the President may be right in how he reads the Constitution. But he may also be wrong. And if he is wrong, who is there to tell him so? And if there is no one, then the President, of course, is free to pursue his course of erroneous interpretations. What then becomes of our constitutional form of government?"

The time races. Near the end of my argument, I kept an eye on the red light directly in front of me, which would signal that my hour was up. When the light flashes, a lawyer is expected to finish as gracefully as he could—usually when he could come to a period. But it was not unusual for Earl Warren to lean over the bench and ask, gently, "Would another minute help?"

I was not especially pleased with my performance. I felt a slight frustration, a letdown. I felt the flow of my argument had been lost; that my responsibility to place at rest the problems of jurisdiction kept me from making as fully as I should have the points that went to the heart of the case.

I brooded over this analysis the rest of that day. Then I realized that I had never argued a case but that I did not wake up in the middle of the night, the next day or two, and wonder why I had failed to deal with certain issues or had overlooked points in my favor. The greatest arguments that any trial lawyer makes are always those that come to mind twenty-four to forty-eight hours after the conclusion of the trial.

The decision of the Supreme Court was handed down on July 24, 1974. Never in the twentieth century had the Court sat so late in the summer. As they had the night before the arguments, people had formed a long line outside the building, some of them spending the night in sleeping bags, hoping to find a seat in the small section open to the public. Many of them were law students.

The favorable verdict of the Court was a tremendous relief to me. I had expected to win. But the unanimous opinion of the Court was crucial. Anything less, and Richard Nixon might not have been held accountable for Watergate. Even a four-to-four split (with Mr. Justice Rehnquist disqualified) would have upheld the ruling we had won in the trial court. But that division would have been claimed as a victory by Nixon and surely seen as such by his supporters. With a five-to-three verdict he would then have argued that the decision was not sufficiently conclusive on the issue of executive privilege. He would have been en couraged to defy the Court because he "owed it to the Constitution and to the future of our national security" to refuse to surrender the tape recordings. This, of course, would have thrown the entire case into a maelstrom of confusion.

If the White House had won the tapes case, the Watergate special prosecutor's office would have been effectively out of business. And if the vote had been so close as to encourage Nixon to defy the Court? The nation would have been even more divided. But enough disorder would have resulted to make an impeachment vote unlikely before the end of his second term. The doomsday conversations of June 23, 1972—connecting Nixon to the cover-up no later than six days after the break-in—might have remained unheard.

Thankfully, that scenario was avoided. Nixon had no choice but to release the tapes. It was the final turn of the screw. The decision was written by the man the President had appointed as Chief Justice, and joined in by two of his appointees. The Supreme Court case was the blow that sealed Nixon's fate. Once the decision was made, its impact was virtually lost in the rush of more volatile, human events. But the decision was historic. The justices ruled that we had the "standing" to take the President to court; that our subpoena was proper; that there can be no absolute executive privilege in a criminal case. They also answered, for now, the larger question of who decides what the law is.

Assured that the remaining Watergate tapes would be released, we could now go forward with the cover-up trial. Had the Supreme Court not held in our favor, this case probably could not have gone to trial. The defendants—notably H. R. Haldeman, John Ehrlichman, and John Mitchell—were entitled by law to the evidence in the possession of the prosecution. Technically, the Watergate task force was considered a part of the executive branch, and in technical possession of the tape recordings Mr. Nixon then held to himself. Another small Watergate irony.

Richard Nixon hoped that the reshaping of the Supreme Court would be one of the major achievements of his presidency. In the end, the Burger Court cast the votes that released the evidence that turned him out of office.

Once he resigned, I had to weigh a decision that had loomed over these proceedings like a mountain. The grand jury had grounds to indict Nixon on charges of perjury, bribery, and obstruction of justice. But could we move against him without endangering the cover-up trial of the top White House aides? An indictment of the President would have meant a clear postponement and, eventually, perhaps no trial at all.

I asked several members of my staff to submit their opinions. Nearly all recommended indictment and prosecution

—with some variations. A letter from George Frampton turned out to be prophetic. In it he wrote:

> The prospect of Mr. Nixon publishing his memoirs (and thereby adding several million dollars to his net worth) should remind us that, unlike his aides who are convicted of crimes, Mr. Nixon will have the "last say" about his own role in Watergate if he is not prosecuted. . . .

As my office debated these matters, President Ford, on September 8, 1974, pardoned Richard Nixon. The question of indicting the thirty-seventh President became moot. On October 12, after almost a year as the Watergate special prosecutor, I resigned and went home to Texas.

10

The Ex-President

Abruptly on that Wednesday afternoon in May of 1977,
I was forced to change my plans. I had just received word at
my law office that the news people were overrunning my
front lawn, thick as crickets. Reporters and photographers
milled around the driveway and trampled the flower beds.

That night Richard Nixon was to resurface on national
television, in the first of his interviews with the British personality David Frost. The press had staked out my house,
routinely, in the hope of getting a reaction from the former
Watergate prosecutor. It was almost like old times.

I telephoned my son, Joseph, a partner in a law firm a
few blocks away, and asked him to pick up his mother.
There was no way that I could stop off at home without
being hit with questions I did not want to answer, at least
not without reflection. I would drive directly to Joe's. The
Jaworskis had decided to gather there for an early Mother's
Day dinner. And to watch Nixon.

I was pleased to be spending this evening with my children, and grandchildren. Their generation, more than mine, had been touched by the lessons of Watergate. And I thought about Richard Nixon's family. Alexander Haig, Nixon's chief of staff, had told me that the hardest part of his job was convincing the daughters, Julie and Tricia, that their father had to resign. On this point, more than any other, the former President had my sympathy. His family believed he had been slandered by his enemies, and Nixon shielded them from the truth until the very end. No man can admit easily to his wife and daughters that he had deceived them.

I was feeling vaguely distracted—I had even forgotten my son's address—when I finally arrived at Joe's home in a quiet, wooded, pastoral section of Houston called Hudson on Memorial. I brought with me a yellow, legal-size notepad, prepared to take notes. Newsweek magazine had asked me to assess Nixon's performance. I had agreed as a favor to Jim Doyle, then on the magazine's staff, but my press secretary during the Watergate months. My feelings about this assignment were mixed. I had no vendetta to wage with Richard Nixon. But if the former President attempted to torture the truth, as he had in the past, I could not let it go unchallenged.

For months there had been a massive lack of interest in the TV series Frost had promoted. I had heard people talk about it as they would a mass inoculation for swine flu. Who needed it? Most of them were hoping they could ignore the shows. But timely and selective news leaks had teased the public's curiosity. Almost against my better instinct, I found myself looking forward to Nixon's appearance.

With my yellow legal pad in my lap, I watched and listened as Nixon responded to the questions Frost asked— and a few he did not ask. My emotions ranged from disbelief to pity to anger to frustration. I could not resist, at times, talking back to the TV screen. What *was* he saying? "*I screwed up terribly*" has a ring of regret, but is not an admission of guilt. Most of all, I was struck by the irony of Richard Nixon's now answering questions he had avoided for so long—not in a court of law, not under oath, but on a television show, for compensation expected to exceed a million dollars. The contract with Frost, coincidentally, had been signed one year to the day after Nixon's resignation as President.

Through most of his answers echoed the familiar refrain: he committed no criminal wrong; but if he did, others had done so before him. And then a new and novel argument: his presidency failed in the end because he was, in effect, too nice to deal ruthlessly with his wayward aides.

One was reminded of the classic Mae West line, when a friend inquired, "Goodness, where did you get that fur coat?" And Miss West replied, "Goodness had nothing to do with it."

Nixon's last defense, against those collective sins that became known as Watergate, must have confounded constitutional scholars everywhere. He defined a sort of Nixon doctrine: "It isn't illegal if the President does it."

I have thought about the tragedy of Richard Nixon often, since I left Washington in August of 1974. I am disappointed. To say that mistakes were made is not enough. To deny impeachable acts and criminal wrongdoing is untruthful.

Nixon did commit criminal acts. And he lied about them. These were not press conference evasions, tricks of the memory, or slips of the tongue. They were calculated, polished, rehearsed untruths from a President who, more than once, had faced the nation on television and said, "Tonight I speak to you from the heart. . . ."

Nixon sees himself today, as he did in 1974, as a victim: of the news media, of the liberals, of his own staff and former friends and, of course, the special prosecutor's office. I noted yet another irony. While his defenders continue to plead to "put Watergate behind us" and to leave the man in peace, it is Nixon who has brought those sordid events back to view, and forced his own public judgment once and again.

At times, the night of the Frost interview, I would close my eyes and concentrate on the voice, the Nixon professional voice, not always the one I heard for endless hours on the White House tapes. On television, and in his public appearances, Nixon's voice acquires a projection, a billowy tone not uncommon to some platform speakers.

But on the tapes his voice had a different range. He was tense, strained, hesitant. He would break off in mid-word, or his voice would rise in excitement.

Nixon's diehard supporters need to believe in him—to believe, actually, in themselves, and their judgment. But one cannot listen to those tapes, or study the transcripts, and avoid the conclusion that a paranoid and vindictive man had dishonored the presidency.

On television, and in print, Nixon has shown a remarkable capacity for putting the best interpretation on the lowest kind of act. I can still hear his voice as he planned the framing of John Dean, his former counsel, scheming in the Oval Office with Bob Haldeman and John Ehrlichman. How casually they talked about destroying Dean, of covering their own tracks, of saving their skins. That revealing transcript, of conversations that took place on April 25, 1973, was one largely overlooked in the deluge of Watergate exposures:

P. . . . We have to remember what our, what the line is, and the line has got to be, "I was conducting an investigation and finding out what, where this thing went."

H. Well, see, that's the other way to destroy Dean, is not only by [Henry] Petersen trapping him but by the President . . . That, uh, you can get out and take the following steps. You can talk, that's the obvious answer is always the President goes out on TV, talks to the people. Well, let's say at some point you have to do that. Okay? You hit them that you're their leader, or you present yourself as their leader in time of crisis, even when it's your own crisis. And that they've gotta understand and share the agony that you've been going through. That you can and must suspend, uh, take the resignation of John Dean. You can't operate the presidency by threat. You don't say this, but this is what you gotta do. You have to remove the threat in order to do it and you say that is what you've done. That, this is a man who's disserved you.

E. The American people—you gotta go on the assumption that the American people want to believe in their President.

Hush money, the pressure to pay off the Watergate plumbers for their silence, was behind this conversation. John Dean had foreseen the unraveling of the cover-up, had indicated he would co-operate with the Justice Department—he was talking to Henry Petersen—and was soon to testify before the grand jury. Nixon and his aides were floundering. The existence of the tapes was not yet known. In the meantime, they would appeal to the gullibility of the American public.

Total immunity for Dean was never considered. His was a case of plea bargaining. He pleaded guilty to a felony and other charges were not pressed. Yet the idea of Dean receiving immunity from prosecution, and spilling what he knew about the scandal, clearly obsessed the Nixon inner circle.

H. . . . the point is if you give immunity to Dean . . .

P. He's a major guy.

H. Then what you're doing is saying he is a little guy. . . . And, therefore, there are [bigger] guys. Now they don't need Dean's immunity to make Mitchell. There are no other major people than Mit—, than Dean, except Ehrlichman, Haldeman . . . and you.

P. Right.

H. They've already got Mitchell. So the only thing you

can give him immunity for and the only reason they can justify immunity is if they nail someone above him. Otherwise the immunity was a cover-up.

Suddenly, Nixon's voice leaped. The tape was turning no faster than his own mind. A cover-up. If Dean received immunity from the Justice Department, the White House could claim it was a cover-up. But why? For whom? Alternately, Nixon feared John Dean and scoffed at him. He knew Dean could tie him to criminal acts. But would Dean be believed?

H. . . . You need to know what John has. But, uh, you know, your "*I know*" was almost lost in the thing. He, he was going on, you injected, "I know." He had to be damn alert to have remembered that and put it down.

P. Right.

H. And you gotta assume that maybe he was, but, but the odds are very much against it. . . . Unless he's got a tape or something else. But I just don't—I do not accept that as even a remote possibility.

P. I just can't believe that anybody, that even John Dean, would come into this office with a tape recorder.

H. And I think if he did, that's one more discrediting thing on him. I mean, you just make the point that that's inconceivable, that a man . . .

The Nixon revisionist literature, including his own, appeared faster than many expected. Shrewdly, his re-emergence from San Clemente, from his self-imposed "house arrest," has been designed the only way it could be. Slowly, infrequently, distantly. On television. In print. At a funeral. In the armory of a small, isolated, partisan town. In foreign lands. Nixon is like a closet plant, able to grow in the shadows but unable to tolerate direct sunlight.

There will be no Nixon comeback, at least as a political figure. To attempt one would be to remind the country of why he went away, and to raise and recirculate the questions he cannot or will not face. Fair or not, isolation is his penance. Of course, he is free to enjoy the not inconsiderable benefits of his years in high office. And to live in peace and privacy. That choice is up to him.

I do not believe in the persecution of Richard Nixon. Yet the record speaks to me too clearly to see him reclaimed as a mislaid national resource, a leader toppled by fluke.

To me, listening again to the Watergate tapes, or rereading the transcripts, is like walking through a graveyard. But anyone who still clings to the notion that Nixon was undone by his enemies can turn to nearly any page, any conversation, to see the plotting and conniving and abuse of power that made Watergate a scandal unique in American history.

He was not hounded from office. This complaint, of course, is still popular among a hard core of Nixon apologists who would not believe him guilty if he had been caught holding a flashlight for the Cubans. He was not brought down by an accumulation of minor offenses.

Nixon's established guilt is not comparable to the gossip that attaches to other Presidents, dating back to Jefferson. Dirty tricks of any kind are not to be admired. But they do not equate with acts of obstruction of justice and perjury. In its final report, the Watergate task force pointed out that some offenses have gone on over a period of time that should not have. But law is based on reasonable proof. The abuses of power, on the scale practiced by the Nixon White House, did begin with Watergate. Some of these misdeeds were without record in the history of this government. Not to win a war or to thwart a crime, but for political and personal gain. There are tape recordings unrelated to Watergate that have still not become public, but eventually may, that will show even more clearly the extent to which Richard Nixon abused his office.

It would have been unthinkable to have allowed Nixon to continue in office, revealed as a President who obstructed justice, encouraged perjury, and persistently lied about his actions. Had he not resigned, he would have been impeached.

My job was to prosecute the Watergate cover-up, not to persecute Richard Nixon. I know, at each extreme, that there are those who are not satisfied in either respect. Some contend he was punished not enough, others that he suffered too much. But the punishment in this case uniquely fit the crime: he lost the presidency of the United States.

When I left Washington in 1974, after President Ford pardoned Nixon, I felt that the essential and major Watergate story was known. With the passage of time, however, certain opinions have hardened, and I have formed conclusions I could not have expressed then.

I believed at the time, and am more convinced now, that

Nixon could not have received a fair trial. I am distressed by his inability to admit his guilt, to purge himself (and us). But I could not pander to those who, living in an island of ill will, have convinced themselves that Nixon is not entitled to his constitutional rights. He may have abused the rights of others. But any denial erodes the process as surely as another.

Finally, one faced the physical problem of trying a former President. Courtrooms are not designed for such a trial. How would a jury be sworn? Who would be admitted into the courtroom? How would the President have been protected against attempts on his life? Would everyone have been subjected to a physical search?

And how would we appear in the eyes of the world, hauling into court the former head of our government on a charge as vague to some other societies—but so crucial to our own—as obstruction of justice?

I was criticized by some in the press for the two decisions that went to the center of the Watergate ordeal: not to indict Nixon, and not to attack his pardon by President Ford. The criticism was not widespread. I felt less troubled by it than frustrated, because the issues had not been taken fully into account. The law, and my conscience, were clear. I would make the same decisions now, in the same way, for the same reasons.

The question of whether Nixon should be indicted arose at two different points. The first was in March of 1974, when the federal grand jury indicted seven of his closest associates. Later, the foreman was quoted as saying the jurors had wanted to include Nixon. Had I allowed it, the vote

to do so would have been twenty-three to none. But I
doubted, and so did the top echelon of my staff, that a sitting President could be indicted for an offense no greater
than obstruction of justice. Nixon was named an unindicted
co-conspirator, an action not disclosed until the case of the
Watergate tapes went to the Supreme Court.

It was also my conviction that the Supreme Court would
not permit an indictment to be returned while the President was the object of an impeachment proceeding. An individual accused of culpable wrongdoing may not be tried
in two forums at the same time. Any such attempt would
have violated Nixon's rights, and I was convinced that the
Court would have forced us to decide which of the two
processes to pursue.

After Nixon's resignation, the indictment question posed
itself again, but under a new set of circumstances. The
cover-up trial was about to begin. To indict Nixon before a
jury had been selected, and sequestered, surely would have
meant a continuance of that case on the grounds of prejudicial publicity. The impact of the headlines describing the
ex-President's indictment would have been impossible to
calculate.

Once the jury in the cover-up trial was sequestered, I
would have been able to move to indict Richard Nixon,
leaving to the discretion of the court the issue of a fair
trial. Certainly any judge would have raised that issue. As
an officer of the court, I would have felt compelled to say
that the case would have to stay in status quo, until such
time as the defendant could be assured of the protection of
his rights. How long? Nine months, a year, perhaps longer,

before the selection of a jury could even begin. The pardon rendered such speculation moot.

Of course, we could have generated instant headlines by preparing a legal attack on President Ford's unconditional pardon. But such an act would have been purely a grandstand play. To me the Constitution made it clear that the President had such a right; that there was no restriction or limitation on how he exercised it; that he could do so for a good reason, a bad reason, or no reason at all.

When I made the decision in October of 1974 not to attack the pardon, there was no United States Supreme Court case that commented squarely on this question. In December of that year, in what is known as the *Schick* case, the Supreme Court plainly stated that any limitation to the President's power to pardon has to be found in the Constitution—and, of course, there is none.

There were some who wanted to scalp Nixon and then burn him without the benefit of clergy, who argued that I should have filed such a suit regardless and let the courts determine the question. I would have considered such a suit a frivolous one. Lawyers, as officers of the court, are obligated to be frank and truthful with the court; we also owe a duty not to bring a baseless action.

Any suggestion that I consulted with Ford on the pardon, or entered into any kind of a deal, is absurd on the face of it. If that had been the case, why would Nixon have telephoned Senator James Eastland, weeping, and begging him to prevail on me not to put him in the dock with Haldeman and Ehrlichman? By the same token, Nixon's assertion that he sent word to me—through Alexander Haig—

that he wanted no bargaining, no favors, was the product of someone's imagination. There were no agreements refused, because none were offered.

I learned of Ford's decision to pardon Nixon some forty-five minutes before the President announced his action. Of course, one could guess from Ford's public statements that the step was coming. After Nelson Rockefeller proposed in public that Nixon be pardoned, the question was put to Ford at a press conference. He replied, "I am not ruling it out. It is an option and a proper option for any President." That answer was sufficient, but as the press bore in, Ford grew flustered.

When a reporter noted that he had seemed to emphasize his option of granting a pardon, he nodded and said, "I intend to." Left unclear was whether he intended to emphasize the point, keep his options open, or grant the pardon.

Confused by his statement, as many others were, I telephoned Ford's counsel, Phil Buchen, and asked him what was going on. Buchen sighed and said, "I just want you to know he wasn't supposed to go that far."

In his final decision, Ford probably acted only out of compassion. Possibly Al Haig and others made personal pleas on behalf of Nixon. But I did not see then, or since, any evidence that a bargain of any kind was struck in return for Ford's appointment to the vice-presidency.

As a practical matter, Nixon conceded his guilt when he accepted his pardon. It is not a document one frames and hangs on the living room wall for guests to admire.

Had Nixon chosen early enough to be honest and truthful, instead of weaving his web of lies, he could have completed his presidency and spared his family and supporters an enormous trauma. Even at the time of his resignation, he could have altered the public perception of him. He only needed to say, "I am resigning because I committed acts that were wrongful and criminally liable. I admit them. I am sorry for them." Or he could have done so when he accepted his pardon.

Nixon might have saved his office by burning the tapes, had he not believed so strongly that they would never be heard by others (and in time would be of great value to him). He would have been vilified, but not for long. Americans cannot sustain their anger in matters that cease to exist. He could have weathered that wave of passion. There simply would have been no other sources of evidence to prove the extent of Nixon's wrongdoing. He could have argued that he had destroyed the tapes in the interest of the country, knowing they contained many discussions vital to our security and our relationships with other nations. This argument would have made sense to many and, given no way to disprove it, would have been accepted in time.

When the tapes were first disclosed, a few writers obligated to Nixon rejoiced, figuring that they would establish his innocence. Why else would he have saved them? Columnist William Safire, a former Nixon speech writer, was one who bought the entire White House line and became a willing source for leaks of a questionable nature. Early on, he wrote a column in which he said the handling of

Dean, and the failure to indict Dean for perjury, was one of the great cover-ups of all time.

But the White House staff knew as well as we did what was on the tapes. So I telephoned Al Haig one day and said, "Well, apparently this fellow [Safire] has some information I don't have, because what Dean told us is supported by the tape recordings. If Safire has other information, I think I'll just subpoena him before the grand jury." Although he predicted almost daily that Nixon would be vindicated, and seemed to have his faith shaken only when it was disclosed that his own phone had been tapped by the White House, Safire did not again second-guess the special prosecutor's office.

I had no illusions about how difficult the job would be, or about the hostility and distrust that would be generated, when I arrived in Washington in November of 1973 to succeed Archibald Cox. I never doubted that the full truth would be brought out, but I must admit that I accepted the job believing in Nixon's innocence. At the worst, I sensed that he had been misled by his staff. I had voted for Nixon in 1972. It is not one of my prouder claims. Nor do I make a habit of opening the curtain to the voting booth. The only point is that I did not go to Washington bearing the stamp of a liberal-Democrat hired gun.

All I knew about Watergate was what I read in the papers. Month after month, I watched the evidence mount, saw the transcripts roll out, the parade of former Nixon aides marching to court to tell their stories. I read the documents and listened to the theories. Most of the facts are now known. A few, none of them crucial to the verdicts that were rendered, may never be known.

My own conviction is that Richard Nixon was not involved in the break-in at the Watergate complex, nor did he know in advance. I do believe that he created the atmosphere that led to the burglary, and that he knew of the deed within twenty-four hours.

The operation was so clumsily done it gave plumbing a bad name. But only one security guard was on duty. The burglars probably didn't realize that they were taking any great risk, nor did they have reason to think they were engaged in an activity that could land them behind bars. They thought, mistakenly, that their bosses would bail them out if any missteps occurred.

In fact, even after I had settled behind my desk, I heard people wonder how the case had stayed alive. Why hadn't the White House buried it? The answer was simple. City cops had answered the call. Once the arrests landed on the police blotter, the long, strange chain of events had begun. And then Judge John Sirica, alone, raised it beyond the category of a third-rate burglary.

I had been warned about Washington pressure when I first accepted the special prosecutor's job. I was not naïve enough to think that there would not be attempts to influence me. But I was satisfied with the mandate I had, and my antenna in such matters is fairly keen.

Only once did I even feel that I was being given a "message." That was the afternoon I was kept waiting at the White House gate, in the cold and snow, when James St. Clair, who had been recently hired to defend the President, asked to see me. An order had gone out that I was not to be permitted inside the White House without an escort. Messages went back and forth while a guard blocked my way. St. Clair was unaware of the order and embarrassed by it. After the conference he personally escorted me from his office. Later, still annoyed, I telephoned Al Haig to be sure the incident was not repeated.

Haig tried to calm me down. "Oh, don't let that bother you, Leon," he said. "My own brother, a Jesuit priest, came by one day and damned if they didn't search him from head to foot. Had to lift up his cassock."

"Al," I said, wearily, "I find small comfort in that." But we did straighten the matter out.

As Nixon became immobilized by the ordeal around him, and consumed by the effort to save his job, Haig ran the White House. It is not altogether unlikely that, in the final days of the Nixon administration, Haig ran the country. He was our thirty-seventh-and-a-half President.

It may be quite a while before anyone knows the extent to which Haig became the acting President. But he is owed a debt for being the moving force in convincing Nixon to resign. I dealt with the general under circumstances that were unique. We were adversaries. At times we engaged in stern and grudging discussions. But I recognized the loyalty of an officer serving his commander in chief and I respected him. I do not believe he ever lied to me. He drew some conclusions that were far afield, and I told him so. But he had a goal: to keep his President in office. And he tried.

I saw Haig at a banquet several months after I left Washington. He accepted an award, and said he was glad to be called on early, because he expected Leon Jaworski to serve him with a subpoena at any time. It was a small joke, but a friendly one, and the message did not go unreceived.

I declined many invitations to meet with Nixon. Such meetings, of course, can be a subtle form of pressure. And I wanted to avoid the speculation that usually followed them. In fact, I have not seen or talked with Nixon since a dinner in his honor at John Connally's ranch in 1972. As I filed through the receiving line, Connally said, "Of course, you know Leon Jaworski . . . a senior partner in one of our Houston law firms, and president of the American Bar." Nixon smiled and said to me, "When are you going to stop putting those liberals on the Supreme Court?" The remark made no sense to me at all. I stared at him and moved on.

I felt sympathy for some of the men around Nixon, especially John Mitchell. He was a gruff bear of a man who had been outstanding in the narrow field of bond law. He was an interesting fellow, cordial, in contrast to the cold and forbidding image many had of him. He went off to prison without a whimper, with a certain poise and dignity. At his arraignment, as I walked down the aisle past his seat, I paused to say hello. He started to rise. I said, "No, John, keep your seat." But he stood anyway and said, "Well, you have been quite busy." I said, "Yes, busier than I would like to be."

Odd, the idle dialogue we create when a man's future is being rearranged. I knew then that the costliest mistake John Mitchell ever made was taking the job of Attorney

General. He simply was not qualified for it. He did not
have enough experience in politics, or in life, and even his
legal training was so narrow as to be useless in terms of
that office. There is no sadder irony than for an Attorney
General who wanted to wear the law and order label to become the first man in that office to go to prison.

When I left to return to Texas, the word around the
capital was that one Nixon aide had told him, bitterly,
"The men who served you best hate you most." I do not
know how Nixon squares that reaction with his own assessment that he was a "bad butcher."

On the Frost show, Nixon's voice broke when he was
asked why, when Dean officially told him of the cover-up
on March 21, 1973, he did not fire Haldeman and Ehrlichman on the spot. But Nixon had known of their involvement, which was linked to his own, for months. It was a
difficult time for him, he said—"heart-rending" was his
term—but only because he knew the circle was tightening.

His reference to being a bad butcher was a paraphrase
of a saying of William Gladstone, Britain's nineteenth-cen-
tury statesman: "The first requirement of a prime minister
is to be a good butcher." Nixon can be quite an actor. He
may have sounded convincing to many when he said, of his
inability to fire his top assistants, "Maybe I defended them
too long. Maybe I tried to help them too much." And,
later: "I made so many bad judgments. The worst ones
[were] mistakes of the heart rather than the head. . . ."

It would be easy to dismiss this piece of business as a
harmless self-indulgence. One can understand Nixon's
need to justify himself. But it would only compound this

sad episode if he were allowed to win by this maudlin doc-
toring of the truth a sympathy he could not have won
under oath. The record does not support him. For that
matter, neither does Haldeman or Ehrlichman.

One of the fascinating tales told by the tapes was of
Nixon's constant scrambling to find a patsy. First it was cut
it off at the Cubans. Then Howard Hunt and G. Gordon
Liddy. Well, what about Dean? Ah, John Dean. Here was
the mastermind, the one who had duped all of those powerful men above him. And, late in the game, there was
John Mitchell, Nixon's oldest and most loyal friend. Nixon
could not be sure of Haldeman and Ehrlichman. He was a
man inhibited, not by conscience or compassion, but by
self-preservation. He was a man walking a tightrope.

Always, there were the tapes. March 21, 1973: "Sometimes it's well to give them something, and then they don't
want the bigger fish." And February 14, 1974: ". . . My
losses are to be cut. The President's losses got to be cut on
the cover-up deal."

Nixon had no qualms firing Archibald Cox, or accepting
on the same night the resignation of Elliot Richardson and
firing William Ruckelshaus. When the time came to dismiss Haldeman and Ehrlichman, whatever his misgivings,
he was ready to let the blame, by implication, fall on them.
It was clear to me that some of his advisers had told him:
"This is your best bet . . . get rid of them and it will die
down." Ehrlichman resented it bitterly. Haldeman was
more stoic. One of the more poignant lines came when
Ehrlichman, after ignoring Nixon's offer of money, bit off
the words: "What are we supposed to tell our children?"

The maneuvering that went on at the top was constant, and almost dizzying. When Bob Haldeman realized he would be asked to resign, he telephoned John Connally. A recent but rising power in the Republican party, a former governor of Texas, Connally had served in Nixon's Cabinet and seemed to have his trust. Connally suggested that the rest of the White House staff might be saved if John Mitchell would accept the blame for Watergate. As the former Attorney General, Mitchell was a big target, and not a popular one. But, said Connally, it would take an appeal from Nixon himself to convince Mitchell to be the fall guy. The next morning Haldeman reported his account of the conversation to Nixon.

In another of those strange third-party messages that puzzles me yet, Nixon later claimed that Connally sent word from Jaworski: "The President has no friends in the White House." Not only did I not say it, I am not sure what the sentence means. Perhaps Nixon misunderstood Connally.

Nixon was one of those people who talk incessantly about loyalty, who complain often of its misuse, but give theirs sparingly and inconsistently. He often recalled—on tape—how cold and callous President Eisenhower had been in firing his faithful adviser Sherman Adams for accepting gifts. Nixon told a touching story about how he, not Ike, had been the one to break the news to Adams. The Nixon version of the story was later challenged. His insecurity, his temper, his memory, all collide at odd moments.

There was the strange example of the Chuck Colson telephone calls. Nixon, working late at his desk, would call

Colson at his home, often three or four times in the same night, sometimes to try out a new idea or tactic for the Watergate campaign, more often to rail against his foes, and friends faint of heart.

Colson told me he made it a rule never to drink until after Nixon had called at least once, because he didn't want to be less than at his sharpest. Nixon, however, apparently did not observe the same restraint. He would have a few drinks as the night wore on, and his voice reflected them. As one listened to the tapes, his personality seemed to physically change. He would with each call become tougher, more menacing.

One night Nixon complained bitterly because some of the men closest to him had not supported his policies, he felt, with the proper enthusiasm. Among those he castigated were Senator John Tower, of Texas, and William Saxbe, then senator from Ohio, later to become Nixon's Attorney General. His remarks were crude and profane. At one point, he toyed with the idea of having Colson fly to Ohio and enlist the Teamsters Union to straighten out Saxbe.

Colson was the point man for Nixon's labor support. He assured the boss that Saxbe would be handled. I have no way of knowing what, if anything, developed. I had a feeling that Colson told Nixon whatever he wanted to hear.

Many of Nixon's relationships were impossible to fathom. Saxbe, at the height of the Watergate furor, had observed that Nixon's professions of innocence were reminful of the piano player in a bawdy house, who claimed not to know what was going on upstairs. That statement may have defined the cover-up as well as any.

The fact that Nixon confided at all in Charles Colson is, I suspect, a measure of both men. Colson made one of the memorable blunders of the whole investigation. I had asked the White House for the tapes of January 4, 1974, suspecting that Nixon and Colson had, for the first time, discussed hush money for the Watergate burglars. The tapes turned out to be sleazy and revealing, but they did not relate to Watergate. Later, during an interview, Colson just could not contain himself. "When you came up with nothing you could throw at me involving hush money," he said, "God, was I relieved!"

Which meant, obviously, that such discussions did exist. We had just not heard them. We kept looking. As it turned out, the tapes we wanted had been recorded a day later. And indeed they were incriminating.

Of course, to this day Nixon denies that he ever approved such payments. In this effort he cannot succeed. On television, he discussed the matter of hush money—bribes—as if hearing the subject for the first time. "If I had been told the money was for humanitarian purposes," he said, "I would have approved it. . . . If it was to keep the burglars quiet, I would not."

Yet Nixon is still haunted by his own words. When John Dean testified before the Senate Watergate committee, Nixon called in Al Haig and said, "We do have one problem. That's that damn conversation of March 21 [1973]." The tape showed that Nixon had full knowledge of the break-in and was already an active conspirator in the obstruction of justice then in progress. When Howard Hunt's demand for $120,000 had been examined from every angle, Nixon left no doubt as to what he wanted done: *"You better damn well get that done, but fast."*

By word of mouth, from our own sources and through the tapes, my staff and I knew what was happening in the White House. We watched and listened, closely, just as I am sure they observed us. It was not only necessary for the cases we were then preparing but also a matter, frankly, of professional curiosity.

I would wince when I read a description of James St. Clair, as I did in one widely read Washington column, as "Nixon's inept lawyer."

I respected St. Clair. He had served on the staff of Joseph N. Welch, whose televised clashes with Senator Joseph McCarthy helped bring to an end the so-called McCarthy era. St. Clair had a reputation for painstaking work. He was considered a skilled courtroom tactician.

But from the moment he arrived in Washington, I doubted that St. Clair actually ran Nixon's defense team. Nixon was his own lawyer. Jim simply could never give me a direct answer. On each occasion he would say, "I'll take it up with the boss and get back to you on that." In every sense of that famous old saying, Nixon had a fool for a client.

I wondered what was going through St. Clair's mind as each day seemed to bring a new setback to his case, based on some document his client had not disclosed. A smart client in a criminal case will come to his attorney and tell him what he did, how he did it, why he did it. And the lawyer can then deal with the evidence.

The casualty rate among Nixon lawyers had been high. First to go was John Dean, saying he would not be the "scapegoat" for Watergate. Charles Alan Wright went back to the Texas law faculty. J. Fred Buzhardt and Leonard Garment were assigned to other duties.

Buzhardt was the political man on the legal team. But he lost favor when, under pressure from Judge Sirica, he testified that he could find no "innocent explanation" for the eighteen-and-a-half-minute gap in the conversation between Nixon and Haldeman, three days after the break-in.

In view of the persistent attempts to shift the suspicion elsewhere, the time has come for me to say that, in my opinion, Richard Nixon erased the missing portion of the tape of June 20, 1972—three days after the Watergate break-in.

It was after the disclosure of the eighteen-and-a-half-minute gap that I asked Judge Sirica, on November 28, 1973, to deny the claim of executive privilege and require the White House to turn over all the subpoenaed tapes to the grand jury. This was the beginning of the legal fight that led to the Supreme Court, and to Nixon's descent.

Nixon's secretary, Rose Mary Woods, admitted to erasing the first minutes of the gap, but even that confession is doubtful. One tends to dismiss her on the grounds that if she had done it all, she would not have risked exposure by admitting to that partial erasure.

Four times she testified in court. Her attitude during her first appearance might best be described as testy. She mentioned no erasure, although questioned along that line by my assistant Jill Volner:

Q. Were any precautions taken to assure that you did not accidentally hit the "erase" button?

A. Everybody said, "Be terribly careful"—which I am. I don't want this to sound like I am bragging, but I don't believe I am so stupid that they had to go over and over it. I was told "If you push the button, it will erase," and I do know, even on a small machine, you can dictate over something and that removes it. I think I used every possible precaution to not do that.

Q. What precautions specifically did you take to avoid either recording over it and thereby getting rid of what was already there?

A. What precautions? I used my head. It's the only one I had.

When Miss Woods returned to the courtroom a few days later, her attitude had changed. She now had retained an attorney, Charles S. Rhyne, who charged that she had not been properly represented by the White House lawyers. "They came down here," he said, "and pleaded her guilty before this proceeding ever started." Rhyne had been a law school classmate of Richard Nixon at Duke, and a former president of the American Bar Association.

By now the gap had been revealed by the press. Miss Woods tried to explain that part of it—as much as five minutes—could have occurred when she was interrupted by a telephone call as she transcribed the tape. This could have happened, she said, if she pushed the record button by mistake—it was next to the stop button—and kept her foot on a floor pedal that ran the machine.

The scene was re-created in the courtroom. Miss Woods' desk, typewriter, tape recorder, and telephone were placed in the correct positions. She went through the motions of transcribing the tape, then reached for the phone.

In the silence of the court, Jill Volner's voice cut like a knife: "You raised your foot." Indeed she had.

The case of the gap in the tape was one of the more curious footnotes to the Watergate drama. Judge Sirica, visibly perturbed, asked Miss Woods if she had mentioned this erasure during her previous testimony, or to anyone else. She said no. She did not consider it relevant, did not believe the tape was under subpoena—Nixon had said it was not—and had been "petrified" by her first appearance in court.

Six electronics experts, agreed on by both sides, tested the tape for two months. They found that the gap had been caused by between five and nine manual erasures. The machine used was a Uher 5000, purchased on the afternoon of October 1, 1973, and delivered to Rose Mary Woods sometime after 1:15 P.M. According to White House logs, she reported the gap to President Nixon at 2:08. She did not again work on the tampered tape.

Could the erasure have been accidental? Dr. Richard H. Bolt, of Cambridge, Massachusetts, the unofficial chairman of the panel, testified: "It would have to be an accident that was repeated at least five times."

Nixon has pointed out that one of his aides, Stephen Bull, had access to the tape recorder, and possibly so did other individuals. But the machine was adjusted on November 12, 1973, so that it could not erase. In the weeks between, only the President had access to both the tape and the machine. And only he knew what was on the tape, and what portion might be incriminating. Stephen Bull was simply a courier. He carried the tapes from the vault to Nixon's office, or wherever Nixon wanted to review them.

No charges were brought against the President for reasons that are obvious. The task force had a rule not to indict on speculative evidence, or to go to court unless we had a 50 per cent chance of convicting. This was not the kind of act—destroying evidence—that a man would do on the front steps of the White House. He would do it in an empty room—say, in a study at Camp David—with no witnesses.

We may never know what was on the missing eighteen-and-a-half-minute portion. The tape was a conversation in which Haldeman and John Mitchell gave Nixon his first hard information on the details of the Watergate burglary. Nixon—strange man—had a habit of using a Dictaphone to record a summary of a conversation, even after he had the full text on tape. When we subpoenaed that belt, the only words on it were: "John Mitchell called me at two o'clock, and John said . . ." The rest was erased.

Although little notice was paid, we found a similar gap, of fifty-seven seconds, in a recording of Nixon's recollections of his March 21, 1973, meeting with Dean.

The paranoia of Richard Nixon would be difficult to overstate. When I sent in the FBI to interview the White House secretaries, and to try to establish how the eighteen-

and-a-half-minute gap occurred, Nixon later seemed more agitated than usual. He was afraid I had found a way of planting a bug in the Oval Office. According to Colson's book, Nixon asked Colson if he thought I might have used the FBI for that purpose.

Nixon's astonishing claim—"if the President does it, it's not illegal"—would be laughable if it were not quite so sad and troubling. The general area of discussion was the trial of John Ehrlichman, involving the break-in at the office of Dr. Fielding. An attempt was made to obtain the private psychiatric files of Daniel Ellsberg, of Pentagon Papers fame. Judge Gesell ruled that national security—the defense used by Ehrlichman's lawyers—was not involved.

Although in this instance, and others, Nixon held himself above the law, he could only anguish over the fate of his closest aides, sent to jail for following his wishes. The continuing irony is that so many of his backers want to believe that he was "driven from office" for being loyal to his friends. Why, then, did he not offer to testify at the Ehrlichman trial, as Ehrlichman pleaded with him to do? He made no effort. He merely dumped Ehrlichman. He refused to appear, to give a deposition, to help in any legal, proper way. The things he said to David Frost, and in his memoirs, if he believed them, he could have said in a court of law.

Americans are a forgiving, forgetful, and unpredictable people. But there are no political roles left for Richard Nixon. In his televised interviews, and later with his memoirs, he hoped to accomplish two goals: to fatten his purse and improve his position with the country. Instead he reopened old wounds and fed the animosity of those who felt he should be serving time, instead of sitting there on television, making large money and talking expansively. His cause would have been better served if he had maintained his lower profile, and let others champion him, pointing out that he had opened the lines to China, and arguing that the good he did outweighed the bad. Instead, to paraphrase his own words, he gave his enemies a sword and then he twisted it in himself.

He is still unwilling, or unable, to face the reality of what he did. His treatment of Watergate has been based on evasion, self-serving declarations, a distortion of facts, and tortured conclusions. He has a pardon. He is beyond prosecution and I do not begrudge him that protection. But I wish he had been able to say to the American people that he was aware of the wrongs he committed and the grief he caused the nation. He has not been able, in a forthright way, to do so.

11

The Congressmen

In the spring of 1973, certain officers of the Korean embassy in Washington attended a series of meetings, at which a lengthy document was passed around on an eyes-only basis. In diplomatic jargon, this meant no notes were to be taken, no copies to be kept.

The meetings were conducted by a man called Lee Sang Ho, but known in Korea as Yang Du Hwon, or General Yang. He was then the chief of the Korean CIA section in Washington. The document he so jealously guarded described a plan that was to be personally implemented by the Korean ambassador, Kim Dong Jo.

The plan involved no less than the attempted subversion of the American Congress. It was a scheme that smacked of a grade B spy movie, with code names and coded messages, the destruction of evidence, and the use of diplomatic privilege to avoid detection. The results were mixed and, in the end, even counterproductive. Yet there is no doubt that the plan was conceived and, at least in part, carried out.

The reports General Yang handed out were serially numbered and picked up at the end of each meeting. In one, agents were told to seduce and buy off—in the Korean, *maesu*—American leaders, "particularly in the Congress."

When he reached that item, General Yang said pointedly, "This part of the operation will be left to the ambassador and ourselves. You do not need to be concerned with it." The reference was to his personal staff within the KCIA.

This moment of intrigue, among many, emerged from long months of searching out and examining witnesses, and the sifting of thousands of documents, leading up to the public hearings of October 1977 before the House Ethics Committee.

Although shrouded in secrecy, the plan, which was to be code-named "Operation White Snow," could hardly be described as subtle. That it was actually put into motion was made clear by the testimony of a Korean defector, Dr. Jai Hyon Lee, the former press and cultural attaché at the embassy. Finding himself opposed to what he called the "dictatorial policies" of the government of Park Chung Hee, Dr. Lee sought political asylum in this country in June of 1973. At the time of the hearings he was an associate professor of journalism at Western Illinois University.

The arrangement of the witnesses is crucial to preparing any case. The testimony of one witness should build on another's. We planned to put Dr. Lee on the stand early to establish the involvement of a high Korean official—the ambassador himself. I turned the questioning over to my chief counsel, John Nields.

Q. Dr. Lee, did anything ever occur, to your knowledge, indicating that this plan to buy off American leaders . . . was actually implemented?

Dr. Lee. By sheer accident one day I discovered the ambassador stuffing $100 bills into plain white envelopes.

Q. Will you describe how that came about?

Dr. Lee. I entered into his office one day, in spring, 1973. . . . He was at his desk. He was stuffing something into envelopes. As I walked over to his desk I could see $100 bills on his desk and also in the attaché case atop his desk, and he was stuffing $100 bills into the envelopes. And he looked at me and said, "What do you have in mind; speak up, I have to deliver these things."

Q. Now, were these plain white envelopes?

Dr. Lee. Yes.

Q. And how many of them did you see?

Dr. Lee. Approximately two dozen of them.

Q. And what did you say to the ambassador?

Dr. Lee. Well, he was almost finishing his packing and he started to put the envelopes into his pocket, and the rest of the envelopes were in his attaché case, which he closed and he stood up and started to walk out of the room, so I walked out with him. But I asked him where he was going. He said, "To the Capitol."

Q. Dr. Lee, do you know of any methods whereby U.S. currency was brought into the embassy?

Dr. Lee. On a number of occasions I noticed U.S. currencies were brought in from Korea by diplomatic pouch.

Q. And how did you notice this?

Dr. Lee. I was discussing with the ambassador in his office, then a man in the general affairs section downstairs brought in a small cube.

Q. A cubic package?

Dr. Lee. A cubic package packed with brown paper and he told the ambassador that this was the money from Seoul, [it] came by pouch.

Q. Dr. Lee, is the diplomatic pouch subject to inspection by customs?

Dr. Lee. No, not at all.

To a lawyer, the leanness of a record such as this creates a special exitement. A lawyer is like the archaeologist who finds a vertebra and a rib and in his mind creates a dinosaur. In the testimony of Dr. Jai Hyon Lee, a familiar name soon surfaced.

Q. Drawing your attention to the year 1971 or 1972, did you receive a telephone call concerning Tongsun Park [or Park Tong Sun, as he is known in Korean style]?

Dr. Lee. Yes.

Q. Would you describe the call, please?

Dr. Lee. The call was from an American reporter in Louisiana. He wanted to know the biographical data of South Korean Ambassador Tongsun Park.

Q. What did you say to him?

Dr. Lee. Well, I told him there is no South Korean ambassador by that name, either in the United States, in Korea, or elsewhere. But the reporter was very insistent;

"Yes, there is." And I said, "No, I have a list of those people right in front of me, and there is no such person." And then he hurriedly thanked me and hung up the phone.

Q. Did you do anything about that call after it was over?

DR. LEE. Oh, yes, of course. If somebody is impersonating as the South Korean ambassador, it's a serious matter. So I reported it to the ambassador, the real ambassador [Kim Dong Jo], and I also recommended that we should report this incident to the home government, whereupon the ambassador agreed. Therefore, I drafted a report, he signed, we sent it in.

Q. Did you ever receive a reply?

DR. LEE. Well, I never had any official reply back from the home government for some time. In fact, none. So I forgot all about it. But, about two or three months later when I walked into the ambassador's office, he was reading a letter. He handed me a page to read. When I looked at the page, that was the last page of the letter, handwritten and signed by Park Chung Hee, the president of South Korea. On this page there was a short paragraph which said: "Don't quarrel with Park Tong Sun; give him a good cooperation."

In the public's imagination, at least, Tongsun Park (or Park Tong Sun) was the central figure in what became known as the Korean lobbying scandal. Some made him out to be a romantic and mysterious figure, an adventurer, half seen in the shadows. But there was less to Tongsun Park than met the eye. To begin with, he was a hustler, a climber, an entrepreneur, a kind of South Korean Sammy Glick. He was educated here, in the Foreign Service school at Georgetown University. He lived well and entertained lavishly, but at the time his name began to appear in the headlines his sources of income were unclear. Whether he was ever employed by the KCIA is still open to conjecture. That he was used by them is plain. That he was an agent of the Korean government I have no doubt.

An insight into the character of Tongsun Park can be gleaned from an incident in December of 1973 at the airport in Anchorage, Alaska. He was a passenger on Northwest Flight 6, which arrived routinely that evening from Seoul.

Although we now know that he was then obtaining millions of dollars in commissions on rice sales between Korea and the United States, he attempted to slip through customs without paying duty on a number of articles. He was carrying a blue and yellow plastic camera bag, of a kind normally given to customers who make expensive purchases of camera equipment or optical gear. Inside were two cameras, two hair dryers, and two electric razors, among other items. He insisted they were for his personal use and were not gifts.

The trained customs agent homes in very quickly on travelers toting such bags. And Tongsun Park caught the eye of an agent named Dennis Robert Hazleton. While another agent rummaged through his luggage, Hazleton opened Park's briefcase. Inside were a number of legal-size manila folders, most of them containing import-export agreements and shipping information. As he began to remove another folder tucked in the back of the case, Tongsun Park suddenly reached out and with both arms grabbed Hazleton's left arm and shoulder.

A crowd collected and gawked. Threats were shouted. After a few tense moments—in four years at his post Hazleton had never been challenged by a passenger—the agent advised Park that he was entitled, as a customs officer, to inspect the case. If Park continued to forcibly resist that inspection, he could find himself under arrest.

As the hearings continued, the rest of the story unfolded:

Q. And did you eventually look in the folder?

HAZLETON. Yes. After I advised him of his obligation and of my rights, well, he removed his hands.

Q. And—

HAZLETON. And then I pulled out the folder, and I saw that it was entitled "Congressional List."

Q. And what was in it?

HAZLETON. I opened the folder and started to look at it, and about that time Mr. Park made a very quick grab to try to get it back. He tore two of the uppermost papers, but I held tighter, and I proceeded to examine the folder. . . . It contained a number of papers; it turned out that there was a list that was entitled "Congressional List," and there were two letters also. The list was broken down into five major headings; there was the name, party, political affiliation, state, committee contributions. And there were names and notations under each of these headings. . . . The list was about three and a half pages long. It was double spaced, typewritten.

Q. And was it written in English?

HAZLETON. It was typed in English; I estimate 70, 80 names were on the list.

Q. Now, you mentioned there were two letters as well in the folder. Can you describe the letters?

HAZLETON. Yes. There were two letters which I remember being from a U.S. congressman to President Park, speaking of rice, the export of rice from the United States to Korea. These letters were almost like endorsements to Tongsun Park. They spoke very well and very highly of Mr. Park to President Park.

In the privacy of his supervisor's office, the agent questioned Park as to the nature of the list. In the column marked "contributions" were either single or double digits, ranging from five to fifty. Park said they represented hundreds of dollars.

Leaving Tongsun Park alone momentarily, Hazleton and his supervisor stepped outside the office to reflect. Just as one of them said, "My God, what are we going to do now," they heard through the door the sound of paper ripping. They immediately re-entered the office, and saw Park hastily removing his left hand from his left trousers pocket.

Park was ordered to empty his pockets. Along with his keys and some loose change, he placed on the nearest table several scraps of torn bond paper.

Q. Did you ask him whether these were the pieces of paper he had torn in your absence?

HAZLETON. Yes, we did. He denied that those were the papers he had torn up.

Q. How did he explain the tearing noise?

HAZLETON. He affirmed that there had been a tearing noise and he picked up a green Kleenex from the table and he tore it up and he said that's what the tearing noise was, but there was only one piece of green Kleenex.

Q. Did it make any noise?

HAZLETON. Not that we noticed.

Q. Now did there come a time when you made a tentative decision, pending consulting higher authority, that you had no reason to hold Mr. Park or his list, and you completed his processing?

HAZLETON. Yes, there was. We looked at the list. We recognized what we thought it was but we, in our own minds, determined that there was no recognizable violation of U.S. law which had taken place or which was taking place by the presence of that list, and we determined in our own minds that it was probably not subject to seizure or detention. So . . . we didn't think we should hold it, but we also felt from the nature of the list and the nature of some of the comments Mr. Park was making that we should refer to higher authority.

Q. Would you describe the conversation you had with him at that time?

HAZLETON. Yes. Basically my goal at that point was to get Mr. Park's full name, passport number, date of birth, country of birth, routine identifying information, so that I would identify him should it become later necessary.

Mr. Park apparently also felt the responsibility at this time because he was asking me for my name and my badge number and my supervisor's number. He was also quite forcefully declaring that he was a true friend of the United States, he had studied law in the United States, he had been through customs many times and never been so badly treated; and while he was telling me all of this, it was laced with the idea that he was going to meet with the Vice President the next night and he was meeting with a member of Congress to arrange for rice dealings between Korea and the United States. He was very forceful and I felt I should remember as much as I could.

Q. In the course of this conversation did Mr. Park use the term "diplomatic"?

HAZLETON. Yes. In fact, one of the better factors about this whole thing was that he was almost as mad at himself as he was at me. He made reference to the fact that he should have gone, or should have used diplomatic—the implication to me being that he had access either to diplomatic immunity or to a diplomatic pouch, in which case anything he had in the case of diplomatic immunity on his person or in the pouch would not be subject to inspection by customs.

Q. But he was not traveling under a diplomatic passport?

HAZLETON. He was not, but he apparently wished he were.

Within an hour after the passengers had reboarded the plane, the agent sat down at a typewriter and prepared a written report of the incident, including as many names as he could recall from Tongsun Park's "Congressional List." As Hazleton had correctly noted, there was no law against anyone's possessing such a list. The list did not represent proof that the contributions had been made. Park claimed that they were "contemplated." More likely, it was a list contrived to impress his contacts in Seoul.

The pieces of torn paper were salvaged and taped together. The paper was in Korean and dealt with bank loans and rice transactions, which he, obviously, preferred to keep private. The significance of that information, along with the other list, could not have been understood then. In time both found their way to the Justice Department, whose file on Tongsun Park was growing thicker, and to the special staff of the House Ethics Committee. A pattern of suspicious behavior was being established.

In February of 1977, acknowledging at last the rumors that had surfaced at odd times and in odd ways, the House unanimously passed Resolution 252. It authorized and directed the Committee on Standards of Official Conduct (Ethics) to undertake "a full and complete inquiry and investigation to determine whether members of the House of Representatives, their immediate families, or their associates accepted anything of value, directly or indirectly, from the government of the Republic of Korea."

Passage of the resolution was a legislative response to what had become a deluge of press accounts suggesting that members of the House, perhaps as many as two hundred of them, had dealt improperly with the so-called Korean lobby.

The scandal was the fourth major problem to confront the committee in less than two years. In short order, the

committee had to investigate a sex scandal that drove
Wayne Hays, of Ohio, out of office; the leak of a secret report on the Central Intelligence Agency; and conflict-of-in-
terest charges against Robert Sikes, of Florida.

The rush of events provided the kind of national attention that the committee chairman, John J. Flynt, Jr., a
Georgia Democrat, had clearly not sought during his
twenty-three years in the House.

As special counsel, the committee hired Philip A. Lacovara, a talented and respected attorney, and my former assistant during the Watergate trials. In turn, Lacovara assembled a staff of skilled men and women to press the
most sweeping internal investigation in the history of the
House of Representatives. At last, the public sensed that
the case was under pursuit.

Within a few brief months the situation had deterio-
rated beyond repair. Discord had developed between the
chairman and the special counsel. In private memos to the
committee, Lacovara had twice seemed to criticize Flynt
for not quickening the pace of the inquiry. On July 15,
while Lacovara was vacationing in London, Flynt said in a
newspaper interview that he planned to propose an audit
of a bill for $35,000 the committee had received from
Lacovara's law firm.

By 6 P.M. of that day, Lacovara, frustrated by events and
feeling that his integrity had been questioned, had dictated
a letter of resignation. This development left the investigation floundering.

Now public expectation, having been aroused, was
dashed; public cynicism, having been relieved, was revived.

Many critics accepted these conflicts as evidence that those responsible for the investigation were not, in fact, dedicated to its completion.

My entry into what was now being called Koreagate was not unlike my Watergate experience of four years before. This time the phone call came from House Speaker Tip O'Neill and House Majority Leader Jim Wright. I knew Congressman Wright, who is from Fort Worth, Texas, fairly well. I had met Speaker O'Neill only once or twice.

My first reaction was to wish that I had been in Timbuktu when the phone rang. My life and law practice had fallen again into normal patterns. I did not relish the notion of pulling up stakes. Nor was I unaware of the potential for failure, given the unwieldy nature of a case that spanned several years and two continents. Most of all, I questioned whether the special counsel could have the independence he needed to fully perform his duties, as Watergate had shown.

On that point O'Neill answered without hesitation. "You can write your own ticket," he said. "If the committee doesn't give you what you want, I will take it to the floor of the House and get it for you."

For three days the calls went back and forth. In the end, what persuaded me was the same argument that led me to accept the job of Watergate special prosecutor. It was easier to say yes than to say no and live with the gnawing feeling that I ducked for reasons of convenience, or to avoid a possible defeat. There would, also, be not so veiled suggestions that I did not mind going after a Republican

President, but hesitated at digging into a scandal that might involve mostly Democrats.

At a press conference the next day, I could not help bristling when I was asked what I thought about the fact that most of those under suspicion seemed to be Democrats.

I didn't care what they were. "If a crook is involved in this thing," I said, "I want to bring him out and I want the public to know about it. I don't like crooks."

There had been some backstage maneuvering by O'Neill to bring me into the case. He had to convince Flynt that the independence I sought would not reflect unfavorably on the chairman himself. Nor was there any disposition on my part to embarrass Flynt.

Still, O'Neill was solicitous, and it was agreed that Flynt should announce my appointment. The press was alerted that he expected a phone call from me in his office at 4 P.M. on July 21, 1977.

Reporters and TV newsmen jammed into the chairman's office at the appointed hour, and watched as Flynt waited by the phone. And waited. I have no idea why, but a problem developed in getting the call through. The somewhat artificial drama dissolved into a mildly comic moment, until Flynt's phone rang half an hour late.

Whereupon he went through the ritual of offering me the job as special counsel and I accepted. I asked that one of my law partners, Peter A. White, a partner in our Washington office, be retained as my deputy counsel. And I again made clear that there could be no interference or impediments to the investigation.

"That's perfectly agreeable to me," Flynt replied. "As a matter of fact, I'm a very easy person to get along with."

Not everyone, I knew, agreed with the chairman's self-appraisal. He has a round, full face and an often jovial disposition. He could be crusty. So could I. Our contacts were polite but strained. He did not obstruct the investigation; he simply would not give it aggressive leadership. In the end, I went directly to the Speaker for action that I needed, bypassing Flynt, to his displeasure.

Flynt had not wanted to chair the Ethics Committee and had twice rejected the job. At the time he accepted, in 1975, the panel had never in its eight-year history taken action against a member of Congress. In his twenty-three years in the House he had avoided the spotlight. He was a textbook case of the wrong man in the wrong place.

In order to honor previous obligations, I was officially to take charge of the staff on August 15. In the meantime, I flew to Chicago to address the annual meeting of the American Bar Association, and there another news conference was arranged. It was again obvious from the questions that skepticism was rampant. I was reminded afresh that I might be moving into a lost cause. During an interview with one television commentator, I was pointedly asked how I expected to get any information from Tongsun Park, when he was safely out of the country.

"I'm not ready to give up on obtaining his return," I said. The commentator simply looked at me incredulously.

Park had fled the United States, first to London, when he learned that a federal grand jury was about to look into his activities.

As in Watergate, I accepted without change the staff that had served my predecessor. The only vacancy to be filled was the one I offered Peter White, who from that time forward was invaluable to me. He carried a large part of the investigative load and performed as a liaison between the staff and me, as well as to the committee, the speaker's office, and others. He shared my confidences throughout the investigation, and, without exception, I had Peter present at even the most sensitive discussions.

At thirty-four, White has an advantage over many lawyers: he does not look or write like one. He is tall, rangy, dark-haired, and handsome, with an infectious personality. No one in our firm writes with more clarity. An accomplished trial lawyer, he had practiced in Cleveland and Washington and once served as staff attorney for the Federal Trade Commission.

Technically, we were not employees of the Ethics Committee. We accepted no compensation. Our jobs would end when the work was finished.

My first task was to learn from the special staff what evidence had been collected. In the Watergate investigation, although it required considerable effort to obtain them, White House logs and tapes, along with the names of informants with direct knowledge and incentives to reveal it, were available to answer the questions. The Korean scandal was an entirely different matter.

Rather than a well-defined charge with visible targets, the premise of the Korean investigation was the allegation that, between 1968 and 1976, corruption had been widespread among an unspecified number of the seven hundred

men and women who had served in the House during
those years. In effect, all seven hundred were under suspicion.

Furthermore, the other participants in the scandal were
citizens of a foreign country. The most notable of these
were Tongsun Park and Kim Dong Jo, both safely back in
Korea. They could not be subpoenaed outside the territo-
rial limits of this nation. Obviously, other former diplo-
mats and present officials of the Republic of Korea who
had direct knowledge were beyond the reach of our legal
process.

The special staff had begun the investigative work in
April of 1977 with little more than a plethora of newspaper
articles—some of value, others worthless beyond the raising
of countless questions—to be tracked down and answered.
The volume of work left to be done was enormous.

By the time I stepped in as special counsel, strides had
been taken to narrow the number of sitting and former
members under investigation. But the primary focus, wisely,
had been to attempt to learn the full extent of the Korean
effort. The knowledge of these activities would allow us
more effectively to investigate specific instances of congressional misconduct. I continued this approach, which involved a painstaking review of the thousands of records relating to Tongsun Park's labyrinthine business, political,
and social affairs, as well as interviews with and depositions
from an extraordinary number of persons who had dealings
with him. Certain individuals who had defected from the
Republic of Korea testified that their Washington embassy

played a separate but no less intensive role in the attempt to influence members of Congress.

One such witness was Kim Sang Keun, who led us to Hancho C. Kim (Kim Han Cho, in Korean style), who owned a thriving cosmetics business in Washington and boasted that he had "made a million" in this country.

Hancho Kim would later shed tears as he testified before the committee—whether tears of contrition or of self-pity it would be difficult to say. He had been enlisted to help purchase the influence of the American government. He was more successful at swindling his own. The evidence developed by my staff showed that Hancho Kim did not distribute cash to members of Congress but used it instead for his own purposes.

By early October of 1977 I concluded, along with the staff, that there was sufficient evidence to present to the committee, and to the American people, the details of the Korean effort to "seduce and buy off" members of Congress. We were still missing the principal actor, Tongsun Park, but negotiations to return him to these shores continued.

We had reached our turning point in a case complicated by at least two external factors: in transactions prior to 1972 the statute of limitations had passed, and until the winter of 1974 it was not unlawful to accept campaign donations from a foreign national.

The evidence of who got what, and through which channel, was painfully thin in many instances; cryptic ledger notes or shredded documents painstakingly restored. Even where congressmen admitted accepting favors, it was not

clear they had acted illegally or even unethically. Some donations made by Park were duly reported at the time. Central to our case was the question of whether Park was indeed under the control of the KCIA, and not just a
businessman. Under the Constitution, it is a crime for
members of Congress to accept gifts from foreign agents.
Then there was the question of a quid pro quo. What, if
anything, had the Koreans received in exchange for their
largesse? The case was like peeling layers from an onion.

There is a process sometimes referred to among attorneys as a "softening up" of the witness. This was applied to
the executive session where Tongsun Park was led through
a series of basic questions. Thus he stood committed to certain admissions and concessions to be used in his public
testimony yet to come. During the latter, Park was not
nearly as arrogant or self-assured.

At its best, a public hearing is a sophisticated form of
show and tell. Documents are qualified and introduced
into evidence. A narrative unfolds, the story of one witness
building on another's. During the October round of hearings, I turned over the questioning to our staff: John
Nields, David Belkin, Tom Fortuin, Jeffrey Harris, Barbara
Ann Rowan, and Martha Talley—all young, between
twenty-six and thirty-five, and thoroughly prepared. In the
handling of my staff members, I followed the practice
adopted in the Watergate case. I encouraged and arranged
for them, under my supervision, to sit in the driver's seat in
the presentation of testimony.

We had asked the Korean witnesses not to mention by
name those legislators they believed had accepted money.

Under the rules of the House, no incriminating information can be presented in public until a member has been given the opportunity, in executive session, to refute the charges by his own testimony and that of other witnesses he chooses to call. In addition, the committee had limited the scope of the inquiry at this point, and anything outside of its limits was not appropriate.

The rules had been overlooked by the news media in its criticism of our procedure. Of course, the cry of "cover-up" shrieked like a siren. I understood the eagerness of the press to learn the names of possible offenders. But this had to be done with justice and fairness.

Through the testimony of Kim Sang Keun, we were able to trace the involvement of the Korean presidential mansion, known as the Blue House. A top agent of the KCIA, Kim Sang Keun had been assigned as first secretary to the Washington embassy. He defected after learning that he and General Yang Du Hwon, in Seoul, had been recommended to President Park Chung Hee to take the blame for the scandal. It was hoped that this step would settle the problem. Kim Sang Keun did not look favorably on the plan and, in effect, went over the wall.

Through his office the money was funneled that went to Hancho Kim to finance Operation White Snow. In their coded messages, the funds were referred to as units of "cloth," and sometimes as "dictionaries."

Kim Sang Keun was to be referred to as "Professor Kim." General Yang became the "Catholic Father." The director of the KCIA was the "Provincial Governor." The code name for Park Chung Hee was at first the "Chief

Priest of the Bulkook Buddhist Temple," and later changed to, simply, "The Patriarch."

Hancho Kim was "Dr. Hamilton." It was to his home in Maryland that Kim Sang Keun appeared on September 12, 1974, to deliver $300,000 in American currency. The two men sat down at a dining room table to count the packets of money. The packets were not hard to count. They contained nothing but $100 bills.

As Hancho Kim hefted the bundles at random, he turned to his guest and said, in Korean, "For our country this is a precious amount of money. I have read in the newspapers that some of the village children go without lunch. All the more precious. I must do my job well." How much had already been spent no one could know. But more was to come. Hancho Kim alone would testify that he received $600,000.

At one point his wife entered the room without knocking. Spotting the money piled onto the table, she stopped in her tracks. Hancho Kim quickly explained to his wife that the money was not his. It was to be delivered, he said, early the next day. And he waved her from the room.

One might pause to consider the irony of this scene. South Korea, a poor country by our standards, a country of hungry schoolchildren, one that had for some twenty-five years lived on crumbs from the rich man's table, had financed a scheme to buy the votes and good will of America's government.

How had such a plan been formed? And why? How well had it succeeded? How much money, and how many American politicians, were involved?

Operation White Snow was to be one piece of this scandal that called into question the integrity of the American Congress, reached into the White House under two Presidents, and threatened the alliance of two countries whose soldiers had fought and died together.

The objectives were to monitor the activities of anti–South Korean elements, including defectors; to "develop control over American and Korean journalists"; and to entertain and influence members of Congress in favor of the Park Chung Hee government. Whether Hancho Kim actually passed any money to any congressmen is questionable. There were no records, no ledgers, to indicate that he had.

In their own eyes, Hancho Kim and Tongsun Park were competitors. Yet some of their funds were commingled. Of the first $300,000 Kim Sang Keun delivered to Hancho Kim, $44,000 came out of an account fed by Tongsun Park.

The Korean code name for Tongsun Park's effort was "Operation Ice Mountain." He was to channel some of his commissions from rice sales to members of Congress, in the hope of influencing their military and financial policies. Given the personality of Tongsun Park, there was no certain way of knowing when he was acting on instructions and when he was merely free-lancing. Clearly, he loved to give parties, usually at the elite George Town Club, which he bought in 1965. He cultivated friendships with important people as a kind of sport. Any reference to a congressman was invariably accompanied by the phrase "My dear friend." He dropped names as though they were sunflower seeds.

For reasons that must be obvious, we considered the testimony of Kim Dong Jo, the former ambassador, at least as essential as that of Tongsun Park. One witness had placed him on his way "to the Capitol." We learned soon enough that he had been there before.

Nan Elder, the secretary to Congressman Larry Winn (R-Kan.), testified that a visitor from the Korean embassy paid a courtesy call to their office in the fall of 1972. The two men visited briefly and then left a few moments apart.

Q. Did you receive a call from the Congressman soon thereafter?

ELDER. Yes. He asked me if I would go into his office and look in the top drawer of his desk and see—he had a habit of leaving the top drawer of his desk open—and see what was in the white envelope that was in the desk.

Q. Was there a reason for his habit of leaving the top drawer of his desk open?

ELDER. He leaned his foot on it.

Q. Did you then go into his office?

ELDER. Yes, I went into his office and I looked. There was a white envelope in the top drawer and I took it out and I opened it and then I picked up the telephone in his office.

Q. Did you say something to the Congressman when you picked up the telephone?

ELDER. Yes. I said there was more money in the envelope than I had ever seen in my life.

Q. And what exactly did you see in the envelope, Mrs. Elder?

ELDER. There was a stack of $100 bills, about that many.

Q. Is that about an inch high?

ELDER. I would guess about an inch.

Actually, the wad was more likely to have been three-eighths of an inch thick, which in new bills would amount to $10,000. Other testimony indicated that the plain white envelopes seldom contained more. It was an understandable mistake.

At the request of her boss, Mrs. Elder located the visitor —in the office of another congressman—and returned the money. She could not recall the Korean gentleman's name. Out of fourteen photographs that we showed her, she selected the one of Kim Dong Jo.

The wives of two other legislators, Mrs. Kika de la Garza (D-Tex.), and Mrs. John T. Myers (R-Ind.), testified that they had been handed envelopes stuffed with money during a 1975 trip to Korea. This time the courier was the wife of Kim Dong Jo.

According to Mrs. de la Garza, the ambassador's wife came to their hotel room late one night, after a dinner honoring the American delegation. At the door, Mrs. Kim opened her purse and handed her an envelope. She said, "This is something for your husband's campaign," and left.

Mrs. de la Garza opened one end of the envelope, looked inside, and saw the money. Her husband grabbed it, went out to the hall, and walked toward the elevators. Mrs. Kim was nowhere in sight.

Q. How did you feel, Mrs. de la Garza, about the visit

of Mrs. Kim Dong Jo to your hotel room, late at night, and the gift of this envelope full of cash?

DE LA GARZA. Well, I was shocked, and I was hurt. I felt insulted, really. In 25 years my husband has been a public servant, which is all our married life, this is the first experience I have had like that.

The next morning the congressman found Ambassador Kim in the lobby of their hotel and returned the envelope. He suggested that if the Korean government wished to do something generous, the money could be contributed to a village school run by a friend of his outside of Osan Air Base. They had taken artillery training together at Fort Sill, Oklahoma, during the Korean War.

Three weeks after the de la Garzas returned to Washington they received a happy, if puzzled, letter from their Korean friend. He advised them that his school had received a $2,000 donation from someone in the Foreign Ministry, who mentioned their names.

There is something absurd about people trotting after other people, trying to pass out envelopes containing hundred-dollar bills. There is something sad and outrageous about the prospect that some envelopes had been accepted. We knew that the Koreans had been sending. The frustrating job was to find out who was receiving and retaining.

Judging from a series of letters to Kim Sang Keun, from Seoul, the Korean government wasn't sure, either. The Blue House sought frequent assurance that the plans were working, and that the money was delivered to the right hands. What Hancho Kim did best was to leave the impression that he had done this. Most of the cash clung to his own pockets. He was later convicted of conspiracy to bribe and evasion of income taxes.

Undated, and in code, these letters arrived in the winter of 1974–75:

> Dear Professor Kim:
> I sent information materials requested by Dr. Hamilton via previous pouch. Please use them appropriately.
> The Provincial Governor, receiving an interim report, harbors great expectations. You should encourage and urge to report continuously on the matters executed and the results so that we may be able to report as necessary to the Chief Priest of the Bulkook Buddhist Temple.
> > Praying for great results and success.
> > Catholic Father.

> Dear Professor Kim:
> Your situation reports by weekly pouch have been reported to the Provincial Governor in detail. We look forward eagerly to the results. Please convey our expectations to Dr. Hamilton, with enthusiasm.
> . . . I am sending some reference materials for Dr. Hamilton and cloths for Mr. Hang Kwang Neun [the publisher of a Korean-language newspaper in Washington] via pouch. Please deliver immediately.
> Please give a message to Dr. Hamilton that the Provincial Governor was sending his words of encouragement and The Patriarch has expressed his satisfaction.
> The Catholic Father has been very busy. Pray for your good health.
> > Catholic Father.

> Dear Professor Kim:
> I understand that you have been having troubles. Dr.

H., rendering enormous service, is scheduled to return to the United States.

The separate envelope . . . which is sent by pouch . . . contain[s] $300,000 for Dr. H. As soon as you receive it, please contact me by telephone, reporting "I safely received the dictionary," and deliver it to Dr. H. without delay.

The letter was signed by Park Wang Kyu, an assistant to General Yang.

By May of 1975 Hancho Kim was beginning to file frequent complaints. He feared the FBI was taking an interest in them. He worried that the flamboyance of Tongsun Park would lead them all into a "scandal." The second delivery of $300,000 was so "explosive," he said, he was afraid to hold it for more than one day.

Kim Sang Keun was not resting easy, either. Although instructed to burn all letters and messages, he saved or copied them, sensing that such evidence might be helpful to him later.

Q. Did Mr. Hancho Kim mention to you the names of members of Congress with whom he had attempted to gain influence?

Kim. Yes, he did. However, more often than naming the names of the Congressmen, he used the words "*chun ui tan.*" To translate literally, it is "advance guard group." Now and then he mentioned the name of a particular Congressman while he was talking about the "advance guard" and so forth.

Q. . . . . I would now like to ask you about another operation by the name of "Ice Mountain." Can you tell us when you first heard of the Ice Mountain Operation?

KIM. Yes. In August or September, 1975, I received letter from Seoul. The letter came from Mr. Park Wang Kyu, an assistant to General Yang Du Hwon. . . .

The instruction stated that I was to meet with Mr. Tongsun Park and teach him how to write a report when Mr. Tongsun Park has to write a report to Korea. The instruction also stated that I was to show him how to use Telex. The letter also said that after showing him how to do all this, it was not necessary to maintain contact with Mr. Tongsun Park; and as I recall it, the letter said I was to maintain contact with Mr. Hancho Kim.

The objective was, by utilizing the capacities of Mr. Tongsun Park, to lead the U. S. Congress in favor of Korean interest. It also stated that Mr. Tongsun Park had studied in the United States and he had a wide contact with prominent figures in the United States. It also stated that I was to receive data supplied by Mr. Tongsun Park's activities and forward them to Korea. . . .

Q. Were the names of any members of Congress included in the Ice Mountain report?

KIM. At the end of the instruction was a list of the Congressmen . . . persons Mr. Tongsun Park had contact with.

Q. And how many of them were there?

KIM. The list included not only names of U. S. Congressmen but other prominent figures in this country. The total number of the names listed on that paper, as I recollect it, was somewhere near 40 to 50. . . .

The plot was growing so intricate that the conspirators

were soon stepping on each other's hands. In August of 1976 Hancho Kim learned that the then Korean ambassador, Hahm Pyong Choon, had offered a sum believed to be $20,000 to a member of Congress, assuring him that the transaction would be between the two of them. The only other person who knew about it was President Park.

The offer was apparently declined. But Hancho Kim complained bitterly to his superiors. He was unhappy because the ambassador had tried to bribe one of *his* congressmen.

Under questioning by Representative Bruce Caputo (R-N.Y.), Kim Sang Keun disclosed that the "advance guard" was a group of five Republican congressmen, and that Hancho Kim made payments to a senator and to an assistant to the President.

CAPUTO. Which President of the United States?

KIM. That took place when President Ford was in the White House.

CAPUTO. I believe President Ford only had one person with the rank of assistant, several with the rank of deputy assistant. Do you know who that assistant was?

FLYNT. Will the interpreter suspend? I will call on the special counsel for a ruling on that answer.

The question was not within the scope of the hearings, and I so ruled. Our investigation did not have the authority to deal with individuals in the Senate or in the White House.

Those matters were beyond our responsibility then and,

as a matter of ethics, beyond mine now. I felt it was premature to identify those officials suspected of violating our laws. What we were undertaking in this particular hearing was to tell the story of South Korea's scheme to buy votes and favors. But we have not heard the end of the speculation, or the disclosures.

Even as the October hearings proceeded, the committee was engaged, behind the scenes, in a conflict of ideas with the Departments of State and Justice. They were concentrating on obtaining the return of Tongsun Park; failing that, they would accept an unsworn statement from him in Seoul. We wanted both Park and Kim Dong Jo, and we wanted them under oath, subject to charges of perjury.

As any law enforcement officer will concede, it is impossible to learn the whole truth about such illicit, consensual acts as bribery or the receipt of gifts unless there is access to both parties involved. Where cash is involved, records are not likely to exist, and neither party has a motive to disclose his guilt. The incentive to do so is usually created by a desire to improve one's legal position, or to cut future losses, where it appears the truth may ultimately come to light.

But when there is no access to the "other party," and no independent, direct evidence—such as a witness or an inculpatory document—there is practically no incentive to come forward and admit any wrongdoing.

We needed access to persons with information who were far outside our process. Accordingly, I sought to secure the co-operation of the government of the Republic of Korea.

The investigation would be incomplete unless South Korean witnesses were made available to us.

For all of the newspaper rumors, there were few hard leads as to which members had participated in the activities carried on, or directed, by Kim Dong Jo, the Korean ambassador between 1967 and 1973. Even in the case of Park, about whom much more was known, the full truth could not come out unless he was to appear and give sworn testimony. Under any circumstances, it would not be easy to separate fact from the fiction he spun.

On September 7, 1977, I met with the Secretary of State, Cyrus Vance, to discuss these problems. Vance wanted me to know that President Carter had written two personal, and strongly worded, messages to President Park Chung Hee, asking that Tongsun Park be returned to the United States. The requests had been denied. For the State Department, and the Carter administration, the matter was clearly a delicate one. Our relations with South Korea were badly strained. They were fearful about the consequences of a proposed American troop withdrawal.

In mid-October, three representatives of the Justice Department, headed by then Assistant Attorney General Benjamin Civiletti, flew to Seoul to seek a way to question Tongsun Park. They were rebuffed. After some thirty hours of wrangling, they returned home empty-handed. South Korea seemed resolute in its determination to refuse cooperation.

The October hearings changed the situation. Ten days after their completion, the House by a unanimous vote, 407–0, adopted a resolution (HR 868) calling upon

South Korea to "cooperate fully and without reservation with the Committee . . . and with its special counsel. . . ."

In diplomatic but unmistakable language, the House said such co-operation was essential "so that . . . the historic alliance of the United States and the Republic of Korea may persevere to the mutual benefit of our two great nations."

The October hearings, and Resolution 868, with its pointed reference to U.S.-Korean ties, changed the picture. The Park Chung Hee regime reopened negotiations with the State Department for the delivery of Tongsun Park as a witness. There was some rejoicing in the Justice Department, which had been embarrassed by Park's flight from London to the even safer haven of Seoul, after the news had leaked of his secret indictment in late August. He was indicted on thirty-six counts of mail fraud, bribery, illegal campaign gifts, and failing to register as a foreign agent.

Two months of bargaining resulted in an agreement whereby Park would be examined in Seoul. In return, he was to be granted immunity from prosecution, and would later return to the United States for trial testimony if needed.

Ultimately this strategy worked out well for the Department. But I was bitterly opposed to such a course for several reasons.

First, I had advocated across-the-board co-operation, rather than a piecemeal approach involving only one witness. The Korean method of negotiating—a very effective one—is to take advantage of an adversary's anxiety to achieve a result and patiently chip away at his demands. I was certain that much, if not all, of the pressure built up by Congress would be relieved by the production of Tong-sun Park alone. But lawyers for the State and Justice Departments argued that step-by-step efforts needed to be made and that such efforts would bring about full co-operation.

Second, I was extremely concerned about any attempt to take Park's testimony in Seoul under the watchful eye of Korean prosecutors. Such a process was demeaning for the United States and would lead to a lack of candor by Park. My suspicions were confirmed when it was learned that the Justice Department had agreed not to question Park about his dealings with Korean officials. I objected vigorously to this restriction, since it cut out the possibility of obtaining information from Park about a crucial element of our investigation—whether Park had been acting at the direction of his government.*

Third, I was distressed to learn that the executive branch had acceded in some measure to South Korea's desires to avoid Capitol Hill. The final agreement expressly stated that no right of access was granted to any congressional committee. I was told by Justice Department officials that it was hoped that transcripts of the Seoul testimony would "satisfy" the needs of our investigation. I regarded this as outrageous. Not only was the executive branch taking ad-

* ". . . no person holding any office of profit or trust under them [the United States], shall, without the consent of the Congress, accept of any present, emolument, office, or title, of any kind whatever, from any King, Prince, or foreign State."—Article I, Section 9, of the Constitution.

vantage of a pressure the legislative branch had created, and in a way that was strategically not to our liking, but it was in effect excluding Congress from the investigative process.

In reviewing these events, it is necessary to bear in mind the climate of the country. The media and the public had grave doubts about the dedication of Congress to putting its own house in order. Our commitment, then, was not only to investigate for the purpose of exposing corruption, but also to prove to the people that Congress as an institution had sufficient integrity to do a thorough, honest job. For that reason, it was urgent that Congress play at least as effective a role in getting the facts as any other branch of government.

The committee, through Flynt, announced on January 4 that it had issued a subpoena for Tongsun Park and would serve it upon him whenever he set foot on United States soil. Two days later I officially asked the South Koreans to "make Mr. Park available for testimony . . . on an unrestricted basis." In so doing we separated the House investigation from the Justice Department's, and served notice that the House was ready to go its own way.

An invitation to send an "observer" to the Seoul testimony was refused (which created some controversy and nervousness even on my own part). I did not want to lend the committee's sanction to those proceedings or to weaken our position that Park should be made available here.† Fi-

† Rep. Bruce Caputo attended two days of the sessions (with my endorsement), but on his own behalf, not as a spokesman for the Committee.

nally the matter was referred to the Speaker of the House and I asked for his assistance.

This last step may have been the most important of all. The South Koreans needed to understand that they were dealing with more than the desires of a private citizen acting as counsel to a committee. It was extremely important that the will of the entire House of Representatives, as expressed in Resolution 868, be seen as strong and constant. The Speaker was in the best position to express that sentiment.

Thomas P. (Tip) O'Neill is a large, shambling man with a thatch of pure white hair who looks as though he had been sent to Congress by central casting. He was elected, in 1952, to fill the Massachusetts seat vacated when John Kennedy ran for the Senate. His grandfather came to Boston from Ireland during the potato famine.

He smokes cigars, sips diet drinks, and has no trouble making himself understood. When rumors surfaced that an apartment O'Neill leased in Washington was paid for by Tongsun Park, my staff quietly investigated. We examined O'Neill's checks and, without his knowledge, subpoenaed the records of the rental agent. It was established that he had, in fact, paid his own rent. The newspaper accounts were embarrassing to him. And some congressmen expect a letter of commendation when they have been found not guilty of misconduct. O'Neill never said a word, either way. He never gave any indication to me that he wanted anything less than the full scope and truth of the Korean scandal to be exposed. As leaders of the House, O'Neill and Jim Wright had guaranteed my independence.

At times, John Flynt felt excluded and this led to some of our differences in the later stages.

Speaker O'Neill kept his pledge to me of July 1977 that he would do everything in his power to keep the investigation moving. On January 18, 1978, just after the opening of the second session of Congress, O'Neill met with the new ambassador from South Korea, Kim Yong Shik, to make a personal plea that Tongsun Park be returned to the United States to appear, without restraints, before the committee. The Speaker made it clear that he expected the ambassador to relay his message to the appropriate officials in Seoul and to report back to him upon his return. On January 31 Ambassador Kim flew back to Washington to inform the Speaker that Park would be made available as requested.

Park began testifying in executive session, under oath and in the United States, on February 28, 1978. On April 3 he was the first witness at public hearings before the committee.

The testimony of fourteen witnesses, primarily that of Park and of Richard T. Hanna, along with nearly 800 pages of additional documentary evidence, painted a full and sordid story of Park's influence peddling. Hanna, a former Democratic congressman from California, had already pleaded guilty to one count of conspiracy to defraud the government—thirty-nine other counts were dropped—and was awaiting sentencing to prison. Hanna used his office to help Park become the middleman in the U.S.-Korean rice trade, was at one point virtually his partner, and received some $200,000 in payments between 1969 and 1975.

A second former congressman, Otto Passman, the Louisiana Democrat who had chaired the committee that dealt with food-for-peace sales, as well as foreign aid, was indicted on charges of bribery and conspiracy. Park testified he paid Passman $50,000 a year between 1972 and 1975. After thirty years in the House, Passman, seventy-seven, was defeated for re-election in 1976.

Park was in his usual jaunty mood as he took the witness stand. A dapper man, forty-one, about five foot ten, he had the presence of someone appearing at a banquet. I had to lead him through the tedious but necessary recital of which congressmen received his contributions, and whether by check or cash. But first Tongsun Park seemed inclined to fence with me. I began by asking if he wished to make any changes in the testimony he gave in executive session.

PARK. I think the best way to do that, Mr. Jaworski, if you don't mind, as we go along, if there is anything that I want to modify or subtract or add, I would like to make my wishes known at that time.

JAWORSKI. Thank you for the suggestion. But I think I will proceed the way I wish to proceed. So you may at a later point seek to enlarge or seek to amend, as I understand it. But at the present time you have nothing to offer in addition to the testimony you gave?

PARK. That is correct.

JAWORSKI. All right. Since that time, Mr. Park, a man you described as a friend in your executive session testimony, a former congressman, Richard T. Hanna, has entered a plea of guilty. He has made a statement in connection with that plea of guilty, which he signed, which his attorney signed. Are you familiar with that statement?

PARK. No, I am not.

JAWORSKI. Let me read a part of it to you. I want to ask you if it is correct or not.

PARK. Fine.

JAWORSKI. (reading:)

In general, the relationship between the defendant, Richard T. Hanna, and Tongsun Park, was as follows: Richard T. Hanna agreed with Tongsun Park to use the power of his office and position as a member of the United States Congress to further the financial interests of Tongsun Park and to enhance the status of Tongsun Park in the eyes of the United States congressmen and officials of the Republic of Korea. For these acts, Hanna received from Park substantial amounts of money and other material considerations.

Is that a correct statement?

PARK. Broadly speaking, yes, I think it is a correct statement.

JAWORSKI. All right.

Specifically, Richard T. Hanna undertook to have Tongsun Park become the seller's agent for sales of California rice to Korea through which position Park could earn substantial sums of money and commissions.

Is that correct?

PARK. Again, broadly speaking, yes.

JAWORSKI. Well, if there is anything that is incorrect about it, I would appreciate it if you would point it out. Otherwise, I assume it is correct.

PARK. I am going to express my own opinions when we come to more specific—

JAWORSKI. Well, you are getting that opportunity right now, Mr. Park. That is, I am asking you whether—

PARK. Yes—

JAWORSKI. Excuse me just a minute, please. I am asking you now whether that is a correct statement.

PARK. Yes. What Mr. Hanna did is something that he was—I am sure he did out of his own conviction, considering all the surrounding circumstances. But as I stated repeatedly during the executive session, my relationship with Mr. Richard Hanna is very much like that of two close brothers. While I have a capability to admit my past mistakes, I still like to insist on the point that whatever we did together was never prearranged, and if I asked him to do anything at all, I did it as a friend and—

JAWORSKI. Mr. Park, excuse me, please. You will be given an opportunity to add anything to these statements that you wish to offer. I am asking something now—was the sentence I just finished reading to you a few minutes ago, is it correct, is it the truth? That is all I am asking.

PARK. Correct, partly, because his effort toward my becoming the seller's agent was very small, and I must insist again that I think my effort as a businessman was the one that finally helped me to get the agency rights.

JAWORSKI. All right. I am reading to you now the statement of a man whom you describe as close as a brother to you. Now, what I want to know is whether what this brother of yours is saying is correct. I will go to the next sentence:

Knowing the power of the Korean Central Intelligence Agency in Korea with respect to commercial, financial and political matters, Hanna recommended to the director of the KCIA and other Korean officials that the Korean government designate Park as an agent for the California rice sellers.

PARK. That is not correct.

JAWORSKI. What part of it isn't correct?

PARK. Well, I could tell you my version. As I consistently testified—

JAWORSKI. No. As to this sentence now. That is what we are interested in. What is incorrect about this sentence?

PARK. Well, it was not the Korean government who gave agencies to me on a silver platter.

JAWORSKI. All right.

After Park became the agent, in order to maintain Park's position Hanna continually reaffirmed his support of Park in letters and meetings with Korean government officials.

Is that right?

PARK. I think that is a fair statement, yes.

JAWORSKI. All right.

When Park lost the rice agency for a period in 1971 and 1972, Hanna endeavored through meetings with and letters to Korean officials, including KCIA Director Lee Hu Rak, to have Park reinstated.

PARK. That is a fair statement, yes.

JAWORSKI. All right. Thank you.

The defendant, Richard T. Hanna, bolstered Park's claim to Republic of Korea officials that it was in their interest to have Park be the rice agent by introducing Park to prominent members of Congress and otherwise aggrandizing Park's status in this country.

PARK. I think that is—while certain parts of it are true, I think certain parts are also exaggerated.

JAWORSKI. You mean your brother exaggerated this statement?

PARK. He is not my brother, Mr. Jaworski.

JAWORSKI. Well, it was just a term of reference, one which you employed yourself. We will go on with the statement:

> In connection with Hanna's consistently held pro-Korean position in the Congress, Hanna allowed Park to be included as a cooperative associated with him in implementing many of his pro-Korean positions, including preparing submissions to a sub-committee, preparing a report, and arranging and encouraging Congressional delegation trips to Korea.

PARK. Again, the facts alone are true. But the motivation is not the way the statement reads. I think Mr. Hanna did it, or if I had any hand in this effort that he was supposedly making in that statement, I am sure that it was done partly to promote me; that I admit. I think he did it, did all these things largely out of his own personal conviction, love for his own country, and also for Korea. There is nothing wrong with American Congressmen making that kind of an effort because, after all, Korea has been known—and still is—as perhaps the strongest and closest ally, certainly in the Far East, if not in the entire world.

JAWORSKI. All right. Let's take the next paragraph to see whether you can agree with Congressman Hanna.

> Hanna believed that Park was making disbursements to

other Congressmen to increase Park's influence with them, and to attempt to influence these Congressmen to act favorably toward Korea.

Is that correct?

PARK. I think that is correct, yes.

JAWORSKI.

Hanna further believed that Park's activities with the Congressmen were designed to maintain Park's status with Korean officials.

Correct?

PARK. Partly. Not in its entirety.

JAWORSKI. . . . What part is incorrect, please, sir.

PARK. Because I didn't make all those efforts just to promote me but promote some of the philosophies that I had—

JAWORSKI. In other words, this was one of your purposes, is what you are saying?

PARK. Yes . . . I could live with that statement.

JAWORSKI.

Hanna's assistance to Park in the achievement and maintenance of the rice agency and . . . Park's access to other Congressmen . . . aided Park in these endeavors, and Hanna received compensation from Park for his assistance in this regard.

Correct?

PARK. It came out that way, but it didn't start out—

JAWORSKI. Well, it wound up that way.

PARK. I think so, yes.

JAWORSKI. I want to ask you about another congressman, Mr. Park. You might tell us how close he was to you, too, because I think this is important in weighing your testi-

mony. I want to ask you about former Congressman Otto
E. Passman. What were your relations with him?

PARK. Well, we started out as casual friends, but I think
through the years we become closer friends.

JAWORSKI. It lasted over a period of several years, didn't
it?

PARK. That is correct.

JAWORSKI. Now, I want to ask you about the indictment
that was returned recently involving former Congressman
Otto E. Passman, and which refers to you as an unindicted
co-conspirator. Are you familiar with the terms of that indictment?

PARK. I think I have been made aware of that.

JAWORSKI. Yes, I had thought probably you had. Now,
this indictment says:

> At all times pertinent to this indictment the Office of
> Supply of the Republic of Korea (OSROK) was an agency
> of the government of the Republic of Korea which pur-
> chased and imported rice for that country.

Is that a correct statement?

PARK. That is correct.

JAWORSKI. All right.

> Beginning in or around 1970, OSROK required United
> States exports of rice to use Tongsun Park as the exporter's
> agent for the sale of rice to Korea, and United States ex-
> porters agreed to Tongsun Park's appointment as their
> agent.

Is that a correct statement?

PARK. No.

JAWORSKI. It is not?

PARK. No. I think what the public should know—

JAWORSKI. Just tell me what is correct or incorrect about it. That is all we are interested in right now.

PARK. Yes. Because OSROK, as you said—the Office of Supply of the Republic of Korea—as a buyer, has a certain amount of influence upon sellers. But the right to appoint a seller's agent rests with the suppliers. So what the OSROK has done, if it made any efforts at all in my favor, is simply pointing out to the American buyers with whom they hoped to do business that Mr. Park would make a good agent for all of us, and which was true. Simply, they used their own prerogative as a seller—I mean buyer. So, it is not the question of Koreans or the government agency as the buyer forcing something down the throat.

JAWORSKI. All right.

Between 1971 and 1972 Tongsun Park was replaced as the agent for the sale of United States rice to Korea by a competitor in the Republic of Korea, and this competitor maintained the agency until March of 1972.

That is a correct statement, isn't it?

PARK. Yes. But not just the Korean competitors, but with the help of American competitors, as well.

JAWORSKI. I am still reading from this indictment which is signed by Benjamin Civiletti and by the foreman of the grand jury. I assume you have seen a copy of it. You said you are familiar with it.

PARK. No, I haven't seen a copy, and I am not familiar with the content at all. But I am paying attention to what you are saying.

JAWORSKI. All right. Fine.

Beginning on or about January 16, 1972, and continuing until on or about December 31, 1975, the exact dates being unknown to the grand jury, in the District of Columbia and elsewhere, Otto E. Passman, the defendant herein, did willfully and knowingly combine, conspire, confederate and agree with Tongsun Park, an unindicted co-conspirator herein, and various other persons whose identities are known and unknown to the grand jury to defraud the United States of America and its executive agencies, the Congress of the United States, in connection with the performance of lawful government functions.

Is that correct?

PARK. It is partly correct. But I don't think I really conspired with Mr. Passman to do anything. If I did anything along that line, I only did something to be helpful to American rice growers. Besides, I am not in a position to conclude any legal consequences. But I will stop there. If you ask any other questions, I will be delighted to answer them.

JAWORSKI. It also said that you were—we are still talking about willfully and knowingly combined with Passman in doing this thing, and conspiring, confederating and agreeing with him—

of and concerning the right of the Congress of the United States and the executive branch to have their deliberations and official actions conducted honestly and impartially as the same should be conducted, free from corruption, fraud, improper and undue influence, dishonesty, malfeasance, unlawful impairment and obstruction.

PARK. I have my own personal opinion, which differs from what the statement reads. But the Justice Department and anybody else are entitled to their opinion. But I don't agree with that statement at all.

JAWORSKI. In other words, what you are saying under oath is that you didn't do this?

PARK. No, I am not saying that. When I entered into a certain relationship with Mr. Passman, while he might have had a problem with his own organization—namely, the U. S. Congress—it was absolutely legal for any foreigners to make a contribution right up to 1974. I thought at the time I was doing my level best as a businessman trying to enhance his own position. But I was certainly not conspiring with him to defraud the U.S. government or anybody else. That is the legal term you are using.

JAWORSKI. All right. And then it makes this additional charge, that also the two of you combined, conspired, confederated and reached certain agreements—

> of and concerning the right of the United States, its citizens and voters to have U.S. congressmen and other government officials transact the business of the House of Representatives and other departments and agencies of the United States free from corruption, fraud, improper and undue characteristics and influence, dishonesty, malfeasance, unlawful impairment and obstruction.

You don't agree with that.

PARK. Not from my point of view, no.

JAWORSKI. Well, it could be a correct statement from the standpoint of the U.S. government?

PARK. I don't want to argue the point. But I am saying to you, Mr. Jaworski, as a witness, not as a prisoner, again, that the U.S. government has its own faults like any other governments have. But I respect, if they say that is their opinion, they are more than entitled to it.

JAWORSKI. They also say in this indictment:

> It was a further part of said conspiracy that as seller's agent Tongsun Park would directly and indirectly receive substantial amounts of money as commissions on rice sales to the Republic of Korea which, for the period of the conspiracy, amounted to approximately $8 Million paid by the Connell Rice Company—

Is that CONN-ell or Conn-ELL?

PARK. Well, it all depends on what part of the United States—

JAWORSKI. Let's try to talk about the way they do in the District of Columbia.

PARK. All right. I guess "CONN-ell." The Texans might pronounce it another way.

JAWORSKI. There is no telling what a Texan might call it. "—of Westfield, New Jersey, a rice exporter." Let me stop there. Do you still have a question in mind?

PARK. Well, one thing—

JAWORSKI. I must get from you either a yes or no answer, and then you can go ahead and explain if you want to. I want to know if this is a correct statement.

PARK. No, this is not a correct statement in the sense that, first of all, I received $9 Million, not $8 Million in commissions. Second, the commission that I received was a legitimate commission, whether the sale involves public financing or private financing. I think with the permission of the chairman and the committee, I would like to elaborate on one thing, that we seem to try to equate the rice agency business and also commission with the way certain members of Congress had the conspiracy going on with me.

JAWORSKI. Let me read the next paragraph to you:

It was a further part of said conspiracy that Tongsun Park would take various actions which were requested by the defendant Otto E. Passman in order to help in Passman's congressional re-election campaigns.

Is that correct?

PARK. It is correct. But I also want to elaborate that there is nothing wrong with helping—

JAWORSKI. I didn't ask you whether there is anything wrong with it. That is not for you to judge. I am just asking you whether that is a correct statement.

PARK. It is a fair statement, I think so, yes.

JAWORSKI.

It was a further part of said conspiracy that Tongsun Park would corruptly provide moneys derived from the commissions on the sale of rice to the defendant Otto E. Passman in return for the said Otto E. Passman's being influenced in the performance of various official acts.

Is that correct?

PARK. I hate to say not correct so many times, but in its entirety it is not correct.

JAWORSKI. Let me see if this is correct.

The defendant Otto E. Passman would and did write and send letters, telegrams and cables in his official capacity as U.S. Congressman to President Park Chung Hee and other Republic of Korea government officials praising Tongsun Park and urging the Republic of Korea to buy more rice from U.S. exporters.

PARK. That is correct.

JAWORSKI.

The defendant Otto E. Passman in his official capacity as a U.S. Congressman would and did hold meetings with and did make statements to the government of Korea, government officials in Korea and in the United States to promote directly and indirectly the interests of Tongsun Park by pressuring these officials into maintaining Park as a seller's agent in rice sales.

PARK. There is some truth in that statement, but not entirely correct.

JAWORSKI. Well, tell us the part that is not entirely correct.

PARK. He did not promote me solely for the sake of promoting me. But he did so in the effort to be helpful to his constituents to move American rice which was considered to be a political headache as a result of a surplus situation.

JAWORSKI. What you are saying is that it accomplished that objective, but that was not the sole objective. Is that what you are saying?

PARK. That is correct.

JAWORSKI. All right. Mr. Park, you have lived in the United States of America for how long?

PARK. Well, I have not lived in this country, but I have been in and out of the United States for twenty-five years since I was a young boy.

JAWORSKI. You referred to the fact that you went to Georgetown University. You graduated from Georgetown University, didn't you?

PARK. Yes.

JAWORSKI. You also went to King College. In Tennessee.

PARK. Yes.

JAWORSKI. Did you graduate from there?

PARK. No. I went for just one semester.

JAWORSKI. I see. And then you very frequently traveled back to South Korea.

PARK. Yes, that is correct.

JAWORSKI. Any idea of the number of trips that you took during the time that you were in this country?

PARK. I have no idea. But as you know, my properties are under IRS seizure. To fight that battle, my counsel and his partners enlisted your committee's help because your committee has my life story. I became aware that I made many, many trips, but as to how many times I am not certain.

JAWORSKI. Well, they would average as many as six or seven a year?

PARK. That is very conceivable. Yes, roughly, since I went into business. Not during my school days. But certainly by 1970.

JAWORSKI. I want to ask you about payments. You have testified to these, as I understood your testimony, in executive session. But again I want to be sure that there isn't anything that I ask you about that either impliedly or expressly leaves an incorrect impression. I am taking the names of members who have served in Congress. I am asking you about the payments of money that you made to them. If you will indicate, as I ask you about these congressmen, whether it was done by cash or by check, I would appreciate it. . . .

I led Tongsun Park through a list of thirty-four legislators who received his contributions, or gifts, foremost among them: Hanna; Passman; Cornelius Gallagher (D-N.J.), $91,000, and $130,000 as the unpaid balance of a loan; Edwin Edwards (D-La.), later governor of the state, $30,000, and $10,000 more to his wife; and William Minshall (R-Ohio), $31,500, and a campaign contribution of $25,000 through him to Richard Nixon in 1972.

The monotony of the questioning was relieved at one point by this exchange:

Q. And Mr. Frank Thompson [D-N.J.], in 1970. That seems to be $100. Could that be right?

PARK. I think it is right. One hundred dollars is good money, American money.

Q. Very good. Was it in cash, Mr. Park?

PARK. I believe it was in cash. My only regret is that the value of the dollar is going down.

JAWORSKI. Many of us share that regret.

Names were named, and every bit of relevant evidence was introduced over the five days of public hearings, regardless of its potential for embarrassment. On the basis of the evidence presented, and on additional evidence secured by the special staff in its investigation, the committee determined to prefer disciplinary charges against four members of Congress, and to refer criminal evidence regarding other former members to the Department of Justice. Information regarding current members who were not charged, but who received payments from Tongsun Park, was made available.

The four proposed for disciplinary action were accused of these improprieties:

John J. McFall (D-Cal.) converted a $4,000 contribution from Park to his own use "under circumstances which might be construed by reasonable persons as influencing the performance of his government duties."

Edward R. Roybal (D-Cal.) converted a $1,000 cash contribution from Park to his personal use and then denied to committee investigators under oath that he had done so.

Edward J. Patten (D-N.J.) violated a New Jersey law by identifying as his own, contributions to a county political organization that came from Park.

Charles H. Wilson (D-Cal.) made a false statement that he received nothing of value from Park, despite Park's testimony that he gave Wilson $1,000 as a wedding gift.

The committee had no power to prosecute crimes. Evidence of wrongdoing was referred to the Justice Department. The committee was responsible for ferreting out the facts and dealing with breaches of the rules and standards of Congress.

I felt that we had obtained from Tongsun Park a truthful account, as he knew it, of his relations with Congress. It was necessary, of course, to allow for shades of truth, for a self-serving coloring of certain facts, and Park's own showmanship. As a witness, he was in turn patient, forgiving, and aggrieved, as these samples of his testimony indicate:

PARK. You must appreciate I am not having fun coming all the way here and for the last 40 days I have been worked over every day and night without virtually no week ends, and I think there has been more than just a gesture at this point—

PARK. As critical as Mr. Caputo has been on this case, I still love him. That is on my public record; and I love the way he dresses. There is no hard feeling.

PARK. I don't think I ever felt that I was completely secure. It was constant battle from my business—so-called business enemies, both at home and this country, and then to make the matter worse, always, the bureaucrats, again, the State Department fellows and their allies in Korean bureaucratic system, they always "out to get me," using American expression again, so I never felt secure and it was a constant battle, as you can imagine.

In the end, of course, Tongsun Park was a free man, under the immunity granted by the Justice Department, his future clouded only by his ability to explain the embarrassment he may have caused his friends in the Korean government. Less fortunate were some of those who came in contact with him, however innocently those contacts may have begun.

Richard Hanna's interest in Korea, he testified, dated back to 1959. The actress Jane Russell sought his help with a problem facing an organization she headed, called WAIF, an international adoption agency for war orphans.

Californians who had adopted Korean war orphans were confronted with double, and sometimes conflicting, procedures on the part of the federal and state governments. Hanna worked with Miss Russell's attorneys to pass legislation that solved the problem.

Through that work he became active in the "Sister Cities Program," in which cities in the United States arranged for food, clothing, school supplies, and medicines for Korean cities recovering from the war. His efforts on behalf of the embattled Southeast Asian nation brought him to the attention of Tongsun Park, and into a web partly of his own making. In contrast to the skill of Park as a broken field runner, Hanna was subdued and direct as he summarized the events that would lead him to prison:

". . . I started out with a friendship with Korea and Tongsun Park; I entered into a business relationship with Tongsun Park in a very minor way, which became major, and that business arrangement called for him to make payments to me out of this rice transaction. It was very clear in following that transaction that I had been engaged in activities in my office which I may have rationalized as being in the interest of my state or being in the interest of my country or being as an interest in the sale of rice; but it seemed to me to be impossible to try to urge or argue there was not a direct connection between the fact that I was doing something as an official which unquestionably was involved with a piece of business from which I was receiving money; and it did not take much reading of the cases to make me see as a lawyer that there is no way you can wear these kinds of hats together without getting the thing merged, and as a matter of pure lawyer-like analysis, I violated the sections which say a congressman shall receive no compensation other than his salary for acts he has performed as a congressman.

"Having come to that conclusion I made the plea I did. I had entered into an agreement with Tongsun Park that I would get paid."

If the Tongsun Park portion of the Korean story was complete, the saga of the Korean embassy, as directed by Kim Dong Jo, was not.

The October hearings had been intended to show, and did show, that former Ambassador Kim was active in the influencing of our congressmen, albeit in a less grandiose fashion than Tongsun Park. Notwithstanding my appreciation from the start of the difficulties involved in securing the candid testimony of Kim Dong Jo, I felt that we needed to elevate Kim to the level of public importance occupied by Tongsun Park. Only by these means could we create the public interest in Kim necessary to enable us to obtain his testimony. We had intentionally "featured" the evidence relating to Kim Dong Jo at the October hearings so that all parties would understand his importance to us. Tongsun Park, frequently described as the "central figure" in the Korean scandal, had previously occupied far too great a place in the limelight.

Our efforts to make this point clear were not supported by the State and Justice departments when the negotiations resumed in November for the testimony of Tongsun Park, with no attention to Kim Dong Jo. The emphasis that we had managed to focus upon Kim quickly disappeared. Practically all of the visible activity, including our own, related to Park. I believe that this phenomenon was damaging to our chances of securing the testimony of former Ambassador Kim.

The long attempt to produce Kim Dong Jo may best be described in terms of critical phases. The first of these was a public phase, in which the embassy's activities were described, appeals for co-operation were repeatedly made, and House Resolution 868 was passed. This phase ran from my first involvement in the investigation through January of 1978.

Thereafter, at the request of the South Koreans, and with their admonition that only a behind-the-scenes approach could work, a phase of private negotiations began. That phase lasted until May 10, 1978. After my announcement that negotiations had broken down, an attempt was made in the House to amend the fiscal 1979 budget to exclude economic aid to South Korea. This action would serve, I believed, as a demonstration of Congress's disapproval of that country's failure to co-operate. The amendment failed for several reasons, all of them extrinsic to the problems confronted by the investigation. I was concerned that the May 10 vote, combined with the diminished press attention following the completion of Tongsun Park's testimony, would be misread by the South Koreans as a sign of flagging congressional interest.

Consequently, on May 17, 1978, I took to Speaker O'Neill, Majority Leader Wright, and Minority Leader John Rhodes, and to the full committee, the draft of a res-

olution expressing the sense of the House that Kim Dong
Jo must be made available for testimony under oath, or the
House would refuse to appropriate nonmilitary funds for
South Korea. A dramatic and unequivocal demonstration
of congressional will was necessary.

The concept was immediately embraced by the House
leadership. O'Neill, Wright, and Rhodes helped edit the
draft we had submitted.

Rhodes, from Arizona, was one of the thirty-eight
members of the House Judiciary Committee to vote unanimously on the impeachment of Nixon after the disclosure
of the June 23 tape recording. He is serious-minded, a
realist, not a demagogue, and does not hesitate to espouse
his convictions.

The full committee responded favorably. The next day
House Resolution 1192 was introduced. It was then referred to the Committee on International Relations, where
our differences with the State Department unfortunately
came to be quite apparent.

Warren Christopher, the deputy Secretary of State,
testified that the resolution, designed as it was to pressure
the South Korean Government to permit Kim Dong Jo to
testify under oath, was illegal under international law, and
was contrary to the best interests of American foreign policy. The State Department feared that it might be used as
a precedent for calling our former and present ambassadors
to testify about American misdeeds in foreign countries.

Soft-spoken and courtly, Christopher is a man who makes
even Cyrus Vance look flamboyant. But he was forceful in
his opposition to the resolution I sought. He was a former

deputy attorney general and a respected trial lawyer in Los
Angeles. I did not doubt his sincerity, or that of his boss,
Cy Vance, whom I had known for fifteen years and
whose public service I greatly admire. But my respect for
them did not soften the fact that our positions differed.

I replied that since there was no effort to subpoena Kim
Dong Jo, only to convince his government to permit him to
come forward voluntarily, there was no violation of sovereign or diplomatic immunity. The South Korean government, by making Mr. Kim available, would do so under
the fundamental principle of international comity between
allies, the concept that one ally will come forward to aid
another whenever possible. It seemed fair to me that where
our ally had failed to extend the help that we had requested, the United States should refuse to extend, voluntarily, our economic aid.

On the issue of establishing a precedent, we were interested only in uncovering the truth about wrongdoing by
American officials, and we were willing to follow dignified,
restrained procedures in the questioning of Kim Dong Jo. I
argued that if the same request were to be made of the
United States by a nation that had befriended and helped
this country and that sought in good faith to solve its own
internal problems, I would expect our nation to co-operate
voluntarily.

After three days of vigorous debate, the International
Relations Committee reported the resolution favorably to
the full House. The resolution that came out of the committee was not as strong as I wanted. Instead of promising
that the House *would* cut off nonmilitary aid if Kim Dong

Jo would not come forward, the resolution hedged that the committee would "be prepared" to do so. Instead of insisting that Kim's testimony be taken under oath, the requirement was broadened to include "affirmation, or comparable means of assuring reliability."

Notwithstanding its slightly weaker provisions, the resolution passed the entire House on May 31, 1978, by a vote of 321 to 46. I was quite pleased and felt that the message would be loud and clear. It had, in fact, provided us with extra flexibility in finding a solution acceptable to both sides. The South Koreans had told us repeatedly that the requirement of an oath imposed on their dignity and was the principle obstacle to reaching an agreement. With the greater flexibility permitted by the fundamental requirement of "reliability," we could test the good faith of this assertion.

The nub of the issue was whether Kim Dong Jo would give us meaningful testimony or whether he would dismiss our questions as he had previously as "ridiculous." More meetings were held with representatives of the Korean embassy in Washington. We received little encouragement. Finally our requests for assurances of reliability were turned down.

This last word ended all hope of settlement by direct negotiation, without a positive and substantive step by Congress. Later, on June 19, 1978, I notified the House leadership, the members of the Ethics Committee, and the chairmen of other committees now involved, that Kim Dong Jo would not be made available under the terms and conditions set in the resolution by Congress. On June 22 the House voted to eliminate economic aid to South Korea.

The process of public education, congressional pressure, negotiation, more pressure, more negotiation, and, finally, congressional reprisal, had run its course over a period of nearly one year. During this time, numerous concessions were made and incentives offered. But the Korean position changed only once: when it was decided in April to make Kim Dong Jo "available" under a procedure designed to ensure his ability to falsify his answers with impunity, and to exclude our having any ability to expose his lack of candor.

By cutting off economic aid, the House followed through on its admonition in two resolutions. It did what I believe it had to do. But, in a sense, this action exhausted the sanctions against South Korea that were immediately available. The remaining point—a very valid one—was that relations between the United States and South Korea could only deteriorate if a solution to the Kim Dong Jo issue was not found.

This was a point that could most effectively be made by the leadership of the House, which communicated directly to President Park Chung Hee a desire to send emissaries personally to him, so that discussions could be held directly and at the highest levels. The request was refused.

On August 3, 1978, I submitted my final report to the committee. It was my hope that my stepping aside, which doubtless pleased Korea, would contribute to an opening of new negotiations through the State Department. But I warned that any discussions relating to Kim Dong Jo must be meaningful and satisfy the indispensable requirement that he testify truthfully. South Korea quickly noted that it was ready to continue discussions—then resorted again to weasel and waffle. Convinced that we would never gain truthful testimony from Kim Dong Jo, I reported to the House leadership that nothing further remained for me to undertake.

The box score, at best, was mixed. A former member of the House was in jail, another awaited trial. Two private citizens had been indicted and convicted. Four sitting members of Congress faced discipline, with these results:

The charges against one (John McFall) were dropped; reprimands were recommended in two cases and censure in the other. The full House then voted down the censure and accepted reprimands for all three (Roybal, Wilson, and Patten).

I consider this disposition to be sadly insufficient. It again demonstrates the illogical nature of letting a body investigate itself. I deem it unfair for any member of Congress to be asked to investigate the wrongful conduct of another. In similar situations a judge disqualifies and a juror is disqualified.

There must be, and is, a better method of conducting inquiries into alleged misconduct in high places. I would suggest a commission of qualified and dedicated citizens, identified with no branch of government, to ferret out the facts and transmit them to a special prosecutor.

My basic objection to the present system is the obvious one. No matter how thorough and unbiased an inquiry may be, any time a tribunal judges its own official family the integrity of the effort is certain to be questioned.

One newspaper critic of mine charged that I lacked the "gumption" to go after the testimony of Kim Dong Jo. He contended that if I were a "patriot," I would have gone on national television and urged public support for the cutting off of all military aid to Korea.

I do not suffer such criticisms gladly, although I realize a columnist often looks for attention, not answers. It is like having someone suggest that the key to cleaning up New York City's sidewalks would be to shoot every other dog. It was not in South Korea's interest alone that our country spent so many lives, spilled so much blood, and invested countless dollars to keep a small ally free. The Congress did vote to withhold $56 million in economic aid. To threaten the withdrawal of military support would have been irresponsible and dangerous.

This columnist had been a Nixon speech writer, and at times one for Spiro Agnew. His claim to fame was that he had composed some of Agnew's alliterative phrases, a technique popular among those in the fourth grade. As a columnist, he became a willing purveyor of information that proved to be false or misleading in the peak Watergate months. At that time he showed a high tolerance for official corruption, saving his own moral indignation for the discovery that his phone had been tapped by his former White House bosses.

There was a tendency on the part of many Nixon loyalists, understandably, to hope that the Korean scandal would somehow redeem their leader. When the "smoking gun" surfaced they felt deserted and misused. They were caught in a vise. To condemn Nixon would be to expose their own judgment as faulty. So a campaign began to reduce Watergate, in part, by raising in importance any appearance of misconduct. One technique is to repeat endlessly the catch phrases out of the Watergate hearings. A municipal court fix becomes Traffic Ticketgate. Any political firing is a massacre. What did anyone know and when did they know it?

This trend was one of the sadder legacies of Watergate and I deplore it, just as I deplore the fact that persons still in the House may have knowingly accepted illegal funds from South Korea. When the investigation ended, there were suspicions but no proof.

I welcomed a letter from the minority leader, John Rhodes, dated August 3, 1978. He wrote, in part: "I realize that the final results . . . were voted by members of the Committee. I express no opinion as to the appropriateness of the results. However, as to your own role, I express my appreciation for your willingness to undertake such a trying and difficult job. From the first it was obvious that the job was a 'no win' proposition. . . ."

It is not possible to say with finality that, had Kim Dong Jo's testimony been available, it would have implicated other congressmen. We knew, as fact, that three attempts were made to pass money, one by Kim Dong Jo and two by his wife, and in each instance the record showed that the money was returned.

We may never know how much of the cash furnished by the KCIA reached its targets, or how much was kept by

Kim Dong Jo or lined the pockets of other Korean officials. This was a case where one key witness remained beyond our laws, where many records did not exist, and where many of those that did were revealed as fiction.

On the day I ended my obligations to the Ethics Committee, the chairman went on television to announce his plan to question Kim. He would be interviewed by mail, through diplomatic channels, not under oath. I had opposed that sort of concession from the beginning. A few weeks later, the committee announced that Kim's answers had been rejected. Members described them as "unreliable" and even "offensive."

In truth, the investigation had fallen short, but not by a margin as wide as the cynics claimed. The disclosures had not met the spectacular predictions of early 1977. Yet any such comparison was invalid because it rested on the premise that the speculations were true.

Hundreds did not, after all, engage in this criminal and unethical activity—which does not lessen the duplicity of those who did. A dozen or so were implicated, some of whom were not punished and some only mildly. An investigator, like anyone else, must take history as he finds it. And he must accept the actions of a sitting tribunal.

Epilogue

Having retired for the second time in four years, from what I hoped would be my last Washington challenge, I flew off to California to keep a speaking date.

Wherever I traveled in the past year—and I had not missed many campuses or law groups—I noted a curious phenomenon. Though the one scandal had ended in 1974 and the other was still in the news, nearly all the questions asked of me dealt with Watergate. It seemed to me that the people had made a judgment: the Korean story was one of low corruption and they did not like it; Watergate was a betrayal and they would never forget it.

Both cases were to be covered in my lecture that day, October 16, 1978, on the campus of Golden Gate University in San Francisco. As I walked into the auditorium, wedging my way through the students, one of my hosts handed me a note. I put the paper in my coat pocket and read it after I had taken my seat on the stage.

The message was from the first White House aide to be
indicted, and sentenced to prison, as a result of the Watergate crimes. He had lost his license to practice law and now
taught a class in public administration at the university.
His note, scrawled in black ink on a small square of memo
paper, said he was in the audience with his students. He
would like to say hello after my talk. He would understand
if we could not.

I was surprised, and pleased, and struck by more than a
touch of irony. The topic of my speech was "Morality in
Government." Even as I stood at the microphone, listening
to my words echo in the quiet, my mind wandered to the
note in my pocket and the man who wrote it. I was not
sure what I would do, or even what I wanted to do.

As I moved deeper into my points on Watergate, I in-
stinctively stopped and departed from the text. I said,
"One of the men who was involved in this case is in our
audience tonight. His experience in government goes to the
heart of this issue and what we can learn from it. I must
tell you that I have a high regard for him today. He is a
man who acknowledged his mistake and paid a price for it.
What is more, he asked for no favors or special privileges,
from the prosecutor or the court. He said he found his own
conduct indefensible and he was willing to take the punishment for what he had done.

"I admire him," I went on, "for the manner in which he
accepted the responsibility for his actions. I cannot say the
same for his former employer, his President."

As I paused, to look down at my speech and find my
place, I was aware of a murmuring in the crowd. Later, in

the question and answer period, a student rose and asked, "Sir, would you mind identifying the individual to whom you made reference during your Watergate comments?"

I said, "No, I will not. That would be an invasion of his privacy for me to single him out. He is here as a member of this audience, as you are." I looked around the room. "However, if he does not object to making his presence known, I would leave it to him to do so. If he is willing to be recognized, this would be an appropriate time."

Heads turned and craned. Time seemed to freeze as I waited. I did not even know if he was still in the room, or where he was seated.

Then, off to my left, there was a stir. Not in a bouncy, proud way, but slowly, with some reluctance, he climbed to his feet and looked around uncertainly.

I nodded, made a quick gesture with my left hand and said, "This is Egil (Bud) Krogh."

The auditorium vibrated with applause, a sound that swelled and grew and slapped off the walls. The ovation must have lasted two or three minutes. I do not know how many political rallies I have attended, although the number is too many, but I have never seen or heard anything quite as genuine as the emotion that crowd gave to Bud Krogh, an ex-lawyer who had just been introduced by the man who sent him to prison.

He had been thirty-four when he was sentenced, in January of 1974, to serve two to six years in prison for his role in the burglary of the office of Dr. Lewis Fielding, Daniel Ellsberg's psychiatrist. As the supervisor of that peculiar underground cell known as the plumbers, he had approved that specific, illegal act. Under pressure from the White House, he perjured himself.

Tall, soft of face and voice, a bright young lawyer out of Seattle, his future must have seemed unlimited when he joined the White House staff as an assistant to John Ehrlichman. He held a number of jobs, the last of which was under secretary of transportation. And then he went to jail. His original term was reduced and he served six months.

There is no disposition here to make a hero of anyone who has broken the law. But the incident at Berkeley reminded me again of the quickness with which Americans forgive. This was no festive crowd proving its political loyalty, drawn by music and colored balloons. Most of them were students, some were lawyers, an audience skeptical by nature.

But they had applauded Bud Krogh. He had admitted his guilt and accepted his fate. No groveling. No passing the buck. He did not claim to have found God in a closet. He implicated no one else. His debt was paid.

After the program ended, and I stood chatting at the podium and even signing autographs, Bud Krogh appeared at my side. All we said was hello, but we shook hands and our eyes caught and, at that moment, I felt a flicker of hope. The enduring question of Watergate is whether we, as a people, will learn from it. Some have.

Index

LEON JAWORSKI has won nearly every award his profession can bestow. He has been president of the American Bar Association, the American College of Trial Lawyers, and the State Bar of Texas. He has won the ABA medal and the Courageous Advocates' award and holds no less than ten honorary degrees in law and juridical science. He is a senior partner in the firm of Fulbright and Jaworski, in Houston, which employs over 250 lawyers and ranks among the five largest in the country. He and his wife, Jeannette, have a son and two daughters, and four grandchildren.